The
CONTEMPORARY
WITCH

The
CONTEMPORARY
WITCH

12 TYPES & 35+ SPELLS
AND RITUALS FOR ADVANCING
WITCHES TO FIND THEIR PATH

Ambrosia Hawthorn
Sarah Justice

weldon**owen**

CONTENTS

INTRODUCTION

Welcome to *The Contemporary Witch*! As you begin your witch path, or venture further down it, the practice of witchcraft can become overwhelming. It's not witchcraft's fault. The craft has aged like a fine wine, maturing in its complexity and influence as the centuries have passed. As it's grown, however, it's become associated with countless tools, traditions, spiritual beliefs, and spells, and there are truly countless communities that engage in, or have engaged in witchcraft, lending to innumerable flavors of magic practice.

Because of such a rich history, there are so many types of witchcraft that it can be difficult finding your place. Do you want to tread down the garden path? Are you interested in spirit communication and foretelling the future? Or maybe you're looking to expand your practice and want to follow a new path? As a witch, any of these practices can be the focus of your magic.

This book aims to share with you a variety of those paths so that you can choose which one (or many!) are right for you. There is no right or wrong path, and you can combine parts of certain paths with others to craft a journey specific to your magic. Narrowing down and organizing all of the information available is the place to start, and so we begin there.

In this book, we use each chapter to discuss different types of witches. We share the tenets and a bit of broad history for each, offering a detailed scope for new or curious readers. Then, we break the chapters down further to offer you "focused pathways," which are more specific paths within each type of witchcraft that many take. In each focused pathway, we offer you ways to begin your path and ways to expand into intermediate level practice, with a variety of spells for both skill levels. With this structure, no matter which pathway you choose, you are given the tools to build your skills to an intermediate level.

Witchcraft is a personal practice, and each witch's journey is different. With *The Contemporary Witch*, we want to help you find your interests and begin your path. But remember: Like a recipe, you can take little bits of each path to create your own. That's the beauty of the craft and always has been: It's your practice. We're just here to offer a bit of guidance.

CHAPTER 1

A BRIEF OVERVIEW OF WITCHCRAFT

If you perform an online search for "types of witches," you're going to get a lot of results. There's a type of witch for anybody and just about any interest you might have, and as more types emerge, some of the main types separate into two or three pathways. If you love crafting, there are crafting witches. If you enjoy cooking, there are kitchen witches. There are even sea witches if you love the ocean, or weather witches if you're more interested in working with water. And if lore inspires you, your weather magic may be more aligned with cottage magic and protecting your home from wayward winds and storms rather than conjuring them. So, we can see how one type of witch can diverge into many areas of focus. It can get a bit confusing.

Although there are many different types of witches, they all have several things in common—mainly, being attuned to the energy around them. They feel and sense the storm coming, or pick up on the vibe of a place or the people in it. They may sense a spiritual presence, or they may be drawn to the natural elements around their space and the energy those elements provide the spirit. A tumbling brook in the deep of the forest offers tranquility to the space, for instance, and a witch would be the first to pick up on that safe, calm energy and understand how to utilize it to ease the spirit. This ability is a combination of sensitivity to outside energy, the intuition within to detect that energy, or trust in one's senses to interpret that energy and know what it can do.

The more we delve into witchcraft, the more questions that crop up. How do you know which witch you are? How can you be two types of witches at the same time? When does your practice move from beginner to intermediate, and how do you know you're ready for the jump? Let's first explore what a witch is and what a witch does, then look into these specific questions.

What Are Witches?

Let's get the stereotypical image of an ugly, evil, cackling witch wearing all black out of the way. Witches also don't wear pointy hats, own black cats, or fly on brooms (unless they want to). Witches are weavers of change, crafting and casting magic for a variety of reasons and they are all around us in everyday life. They present themselves any way they choose. This means you can be a sweat-pants-wearing witch or a fashion-forward one, a tarot-wielding witch wearing stones around your neck, or a garden witch in running shoes sporting a mom bun. This is your practice, and you can show up any way you choose. In fact, many don't feel the need to have their outside appearance reflect their practice at all. So, there's no telling who's a witch and who isn't solely based on appearances. But you may get a sense of who practices the Craft!

It's also important to note that witchcraft isn't only for women. Although history and the media would suggest there are many more women than men in the practice, there are male practitioners, too, and they have contributed to the practice in influential ways—from books to the creation of spiritual movements and so on—that have affected the way many see witchcraft, and they continue to influence the witchcraft realm today. Although witches in general may see witchcraft as a way for women to reclaim their space, we can't deny that men have had as much impact on creating the pathways we know and practice, and many women have sought to deny or renounce the craft as we know it. Witchcraft and its practice are all about inclusion and respect for others, regardless of gender.

In the same vein, witchcraft welcomes all people from all walks of life and belief systems. Throughout history, witches have faced persecution for their looks, beliefs, rituals, and lifestyle choices and many witches see witchcraft as a safe, welcoming space to be themselves and practice their magic. It's our opinion that this facet of witchcraft is, perhaps, one of the most important, and what makes the path so appealing to many.

What Makes Someone a Witch?

Although there are many shared personality traits and habits that can help you determine whether you're a witch, it's important to stress that, ultimately, it comes down to choice: You're a witch when you say you're a witch. Intentions are very important to witchcraft. This means that if your intentions are to practice witchcraft, cast spells, create change in your life, or become closer to spiritual or natural energies, you're likely ready to call yourself a witch. However, if you still feel on the fence about whether you're ready to call yourself a witch, here are some personality traits many witches have. You might align with one, or many, of them.

You often have a strong connection to the world around you.

Do you feel an appreciation for all that earth provides? You might enjoy being out in nature, admiring flowers and the changing colors of the trees throughout the seasons, or the mesmerizing force of a flowing river. This appreciation for nature and its beauty can also inspire you. This connection doesn't just have to be with the earth. Do you feel a spiritual connection to the sea, rain, or other watery sources? Do you have a particular draw to candles and campfires? Some witches have specific connections to one or more of the elements, which boils down to one aspect: You respect the elements and feel a kinship with one or more of them.

You feel drawn to the moon and its phases.

Do you often feel in sync with the moon, whether it's a full or new moon? The monthly changing phases may spark wonder in your heart or make you feel emotions outside your normal feelings. You may be drawn to cleansing and renewal when the moon is waning or dark, or you may feel more energetic, passionate, and hopeful when the moon is waxing or full. If you're not sure, use the next moon cycle to see whether your emotions align with the moon's phases. There are many apps and calendars that share the moon's cycle to help guide you. The moon has a push and pull on us, as it does on the ocean's tides, and many of us aren't even aware of that influence. There's a reason many emergency rooms are more frantic and full during a full moon! A witch, on the other hand, senses that connection and is, perhaps, drawn to it, watching the moon change and noticing how inner feelings align with those phases. Or, may feel guided and comforted by the moon as a spiritual presence, one we seek out when not feeling well, perhaps by sitting under the moonbeams or watching it out the window.

You recognize the energy of the elements.

Like the admiration of a flowing river, you recognize the power within the elements. This might include the energy from a flickering flame, a gust of wind, or blooming plants. There's energy in the way an element moves and changes that may have already caught your eye. You may also feel an internal relationship with these elements; some feel comforted and grounded by laying on earth, and some feel invigorated or cleansed when stepping barefoot into a running river. You don't necessarily think about these things; they are feelings that come to you naturally, though being mindful of what's happening and acknowledging it is also a witchy trait!

You perform rituals everywhere in your life.

This can be anything from cleaning a certain way, trusting your intuition to perform certain tasks, or simply doing something routinely because you feel drawn to do so. Maybe you start every day with a cup of coffee, stirring it as you daydream for a bit to wake up. That's a ritual, though it may not seem like it. Although everyone has habits, rituals take on a more emotional or spiritual purpose: They set your intention or prepare the mind, body, and space for happier living.

You have an interest in natural living.

Your strong connection to the elements around you may encourage you to live in a way that respects these elements, like recycling and composting, creating herbal remedies and homemade ointments, homesteading or gardening, or maybe living off the grid. It doesn't have to be this intense, though. Simple acts, like choosing renewable resources and using less water, are also aspects of natural living and may be the only ways a witch can perform natural living, especially urban witches!

You are an empath.

Empaths feel the energies around them, from people and from spaces. They can usually interpret these energies as feelings or previous experiences and memories. This is typically involuntary and the feelings simply arrive in your head without warning. You may also be inclined to help and heal others, a natural trait of an empath, because you have a strong ability to empathize or sympathize with others and their experiences. This ability comes from being able to feel their energies, which allows you to relate to them on a spiritual or deeply personal level.

As you can see, there are several main traits of a witch, but each can be more complex than these simplified descriptions. We'll explore these concepts more in later chapters and how they relate to specific types of witches.

Interests of Witches

In addition to the preceding list of what makes someone a witch, there are certain interests witches seem drawn to in their practices. These interests have been the identifiers of witches throughout time. However, it's important to note that, although many witches are characterized by their interest in the topics following, not everyone who is interested in these topics are witches. That said, many of these topics are what led witches to perform their craft, are driving motivators for witches to practice their craft, or make up a good portion of someone's witchcraft practice.

HEALING AND MEDICINE

Witches are, for the most part, healers. They aren't afraid to try something new, holistically, to help others heal from illness or pain. They reach toward nature to brew teas, blend herbs, or chant to mend. They may also use folk remedies from their chosen practice that are said to have healing properties. And, although not all witches are healers or have an interest in medicine, many take on this interest as part of their craft, if even just to heal themselves (which is completely okay).

SPELLS

Spells are a way for witches to weave change. Spells are energy intertwined with action and intention. They can be created with a witch's mind or physical items. Throughout time, witches have created charms, incantations, or rituals for a certain goal, usually to attract something or repel something to create the change they wanted. Spells can be as elaborate as crafting a protective circle, lighting candles, asking deities for help, performing a tarot reading, and creating a charm bag based on what the cards foretold, or as simple as drawing a symbol and hanging it in a window. Both approaches can bring about change.

MEDITATION OR SPIRITUAL MOVEMENT

Many witches also practice meditation or other activities with a spiritual undertone, like yoga or tai chi. Because witchcraft focuses a good deal on mindfulness and being able to move or manipulate energy, activities like these help with controlling the mind and identifying where energy is in the body, meaning they're ideal tools to help make spellwork easier to perform for the practicing witch. Some even use meditation as spells, using visualization in meditation to bring about intention or to meet spirit guides.

SPIRITS AND ANCESTORS

Spirits, the dead, afterlife, and all that came before us have historically been a large part of witches' practices. Witches performed divination readings, seances, lit candles, made offerings, and gave feasts to those not physically present, not only to honor the spirits but also to ask them for assistance and guidance, or added energy in spells. Calling upon the spiritual realm isn't just to access these beings: Witches call upon any deities they align with, like Greek or Norse gods and goddesses, or spiritual ancestors from our belief systems, like shamans from antiquity who scrawled their spiritual journeys on cave walls. No matter the spiritual entity on the other side, witches are known to have close relationships with them and are able to ask for their assistance when needed.

What Does It Mean to Be a "Type" of Witch?

There are many "types" of witches, as we'll learn in this book. These types are guidelines to help you hone your craft and help you explore it in more detail. They aren't meant to restrict you into any one type or suggest we all need labels, especially when talking about a practice grounded in accepting and including all types of people and their beliefs. Witchcraft is an unfathomably large concept and practice, with a rich, varied, painful, and yet beautiful, history. And, as practitioners continue to practice their craft without impunity, we're able to explore all of what witchcraft offers and entails. Because the craft is so broad, we've provided "types" of witches to help guide you in your learning and provide areas of focus that may appeal to you. Many witches even mix and match their practices, or choose a pathway that works for one particular issue or at a certain time in their life, meaning many witches having many labels. Witches may be, all at once, a traditional kitchen witch and an eclectic crystal witch. Just as we are in life, we are many things in our craft. Don't feel limited by these types. Use them to help guide your interests.

How to Know You're an Intermediate Witch

The gap between the beginner and the intermediate witch can seem vast—because it is. Witchcraft is nuanced, and although there are paths with clear delineations for expertise and rank, many paths aren't as clear-cut. So, how do you know when you're ready for intermediate magic? Understanding when it's time for a more complex, challenging practice comes from an awareness of your abilities, trust in your craft, and a desire to learn and do more. Many beginner witches will start their practice with a select few tools, like a quartz crystal, a few tea light or votive candles, a bowl, a book of spells they've purchased, and, maybe, a cauldron. Many spells can be crafted from these core tools, including those in many books. But once a beginner witch begins to seek more, or feels unchallenged by these spells, or yearns for ways to have a deeper connection with their path, like learning its history, or wants a stronger connection with the spirits and deities in their belief system, the change from beginner witch to intermediate has begun.

Intermediate witches also want to take their practice to new levels, incorporate new ingredients, and try new tools. Perhaps they also feel as though they've mastered a particular type of magic or spell and want to try a new type of witchcraft, and so they begin the journey all over again but in a new area of focus.

In this book, we'll dive into those next steps for witches on their journey, uncovering the many types of witches there are and how to explore their craft. This intermediate guide will show you how the various types of witches came to be, how to get started in that type of witchcraft, ingredients commonly used in that type of craft, and unique spells to try. Before I move on to all the wonderful types of witches, we'll first discuss witchcraft throughout history and how different types of witchcraft can overlap. Perhaps, one day, you'll create your unique type of witchcraft to share with others.

Closed Practices and Cultural Appropriation

Witchcraft practices often walk a fine line between cultural appropriation and appreciation. Often, this is an extremely sensitive subject in the magical community. Cultural appropriation is harmful because it diminishes historical persecution while still oppressing the culture from which it comes. And while some may see their practices as a way to honor those cultures, it actually takes the focus off the not-so-appealing parts of history in favor of more palatable, fun, interesting cultural tidbits that become fodder over dinner. And that's a problem, considering many of these cultures still suffer from the impact of persecution hundreds of years later.

In a more individual sense, controversy also lies in the fact that some are attracted to witchcraft because many of its paths are free from structure or rules. But this openness creates a blending and melding of spiritual activities that, after time, become bastardized, losing their historical and cultural origins. And, many who practice these activities are not even aware of the context surrounding their practices, sometimes even performing a spell without knowing those practices have a completely different meaning or purpose.

Marketing items or services, and using the term *witchy* or other trendy words is also an issue. It's partly thanks to these "witchy" products that witchcraft has become more popular than ever. We now see items such as witch kits, cleansing wands, and chakra sprays on store shelves, all of which can harm more often than not. Chakras are sacred to cultures found in Southeast Asia, commonly found in Hindu practices. Cleansing sticks are sacred to Indigenous cultures in North America, widely used for ceremonial cleansing and ritual, also called smudging. Witch kits are often sold with items from these and other cultures without celebrating or even sharing their origins.

It's important to note that although chakras are sacred to practices such as Hindu, the movement of energy throughout the body isn't a closed practice or off-limits. You can still perform the work. This is also true of the use of cleansing rituals in one's practice. But many cultures across the world that have incorporated specific spiritual or magical practices did so for a particular reason associated with their culture and their people, and they've done so for eons. These are closed practices to those who are not from these cultures. As a general rule, if you don't know where a certain custom came from, take time to find out.

So, if you want to be respectful of closed practices but still incorporate these fundamentals, appreciate chakras and cleansing rituals but don't use or re-brand them. You can incorporate energy work or cleansing into your practice but don't use labels from other cultures for popularity. Help share the context of these practices, good and bad, to educate others on their historical significance. And while you continue to expand your witchcraft practice and learn new things, educate yourself on other cultures to learn what might be off-limits.

Materials and Tools

Tools are very important to witches. They can help amplify spells and make your practice more personal and powerful. While handmade tools aren't inherently magical, they can help you channel your energy or the energy of natural resources. Many tools can be substituted for any you don't have if there's an intended purpose. For example, if you need a wand, use any object with a point to help you direct energy.

As an intermediate witch, you might have already begun collecting tools you enjoy using along the way but are also curious about other tools prominent to different types of witchcraft. In the later chapters of this book, I break down the many tools associated with the different types of witchcraft. The following is a guide to the common tools you might find in overlapping witchcraft practices.

General Materials and Tools

TOOL	DESCRIPTION	PROPERTIES
Candles	Candles come in a variety of colors, shapes, sizes, and wax types. Chime candles are small pillar candles. Their small size allows for a quicker burn time.	Candles can amplify, send out, and attract energies for spells and rituals. They can be dressed in oil (see page 64), carved with symbols, or simply burned.
Colors	Each color has its individual associations (see opposite) that can be used whether in candle, crystal, fabric, or other forms.	Colors enhance or imbue certain properties into spells or rituals. They may also correspond to deities used in your practice.
Crystals	Crystals are great sources of natural energy, and each crystal also carries unique magical properties.	In general, crystals are used for absorbing, boosting energy, centering, and grounding.
Incense	Incense is often used to burn plant material in different forms, such as bundles, cones, loose, spirals, and sticks.	Incense can clear away, amplify, and assist with spiritual or meditative states for spells and rituals.
Oils	Essential oils* are versatile tools in different types of witchcraft. Carrier oils* dilute essential oils to be used safely on one's skin. *Safety Note: Essential oils can be harmful to the body when applied directly and poisonous when ingested. Always dilute essential oils with carrier oils when applying to the body or handling (see page 64). Carefully read and follow the manufacturer's directions.	Oils can be charged and infused with intentions for attracting or repelling. They're also used to dress candles.
Salt	There are many types of salt, each with its own intention.	Use salts to create protective circles or barriers in spells and rituals, or use as an offering to ancestors or deities.
Vessels	Vessels, often bowls, cauldrons, chalices, or jars, are practical tools that hold ingredients for spells, or that can be used for divination.	Vessels bring properties of creativity, feminine energy, and the element of water to spells or rituals. Cauldrons are often made from cast iron, making them fire-safe and ideal for spells utilizing fire.

Colors

Colors are important to spells and rituals too, no matter your skill level. From textiles and candles to dried flowers and stones, colors are an easy way to add additional intention.

Color Correspondences

COLOR	CORRESPONDENCES
Black	Banishing, cursing, grief, negativity removal, protection, new moon work, shadow work.
Blue	Calm, clarity, dreams, emotional regulation, healing, meditation, peace; represents the water element.
Brown	Foundations, grounding, safety, stability.
Gold	Connections to divinity, namely the sun.
Green	Money, fertility, abundance; represents the earth element.
Orange	Abundance, energy, prosperity, vitality.
Purple	Divinity, meditation, spiritual heightening, spirituality, visualization.
Red	Bravery, motivation, passion, protection, sex, strength; represents the fire element.
Silver	Connections to divinity, namely the moon.
White	Cleansing, meditation or trancework, purity, spiritual connection.
Yellow	Communication, creativity, inspiration; represents the air element.

CHAPTER 2

TYPES OF WITCHES & THEIR OVERLAP

Although a witch is known to cast magic to create change, there isn't a one-size-fits-all option to witchcraft, because many belief systems have one or two tidbits in them that may not work for some. And so, as we learn about different types of witchcraft and the witches who perform the work, we may find some aspects we don't like, or that others fit our personality better. You may be drawn to herbs and the hearth as a means of creating magic, but you feel drawn to help the community, too. Or maybe you feel a kinship with one deity, but your practice focuses more on the spiritual side of animals, plants, and earth. That's okay. All practitioners pick and choose what and how they practice, to create an à la carte craft style and, even then, this style can change as we grow and find new interests, have new spiritual experiences, and so on. It's ever-evolving, and so our identities and interests evolve, too, changing what "type" of witch we are or what we include in our practice. That is the spiritual journey.

There are many types of witches, and many of the types also overlap in the tools used (robes can be used in structured Wiccan rites and by the solitary witch roaming the woods collecting herbs); the belief systems in place (we can believe in traveling to the spiritual realm but not really believe in gods and goddesses); and the source of our information (spells may come from contemporary books by modern witches or from a compendium of Old-World spells). Witches also overlap in terms of definitions. By definition, a practice can be labeled "contemporary" because it's new, "eclectic" because it includes spells or practices from many belief systems, and "regional" because the majority of its focus comes from one region. And so, you can be a contemporary eclectic regional witch. And that's okay, too.

No matter how the types of witches and witchcraft overlap, one thing is certain: It was bound to happen. Witchcraft is an ancient concept that has been prevalent in cultures and regions worldwide, and the rituals and reverence witches perform today stem from practices performed thousands of years ago. And although there were attempts to snuff out witchcraft, demonize it, and morph it into a more Christian-like experience, it endured. Incremental changes over time and through cultures mean one version of witchcraft can be mildly different from the last, or that one version in one region is similar to another because those people emigrated there. The result is something so rich, so complex, there are bound to be similarities among countless "types."

Given this, it's hard not to become overwhelmed. So, we attempt to identify the kind of witch we are to help us focus and cull such a vast array of information, though not to "label" ourselves as much as to try to find ourselves within a practice that's complex. The following is a look at some of the different types of witches practicing today. You will likely fit into more than one category.

Cultural and Folk Witches

Cultural, or folk, practices encompass magic that dates back to one's ancestries centuries ago. Typically, these practices are passed down within the same culture, or from one's family, and take on a strong communal or cultural aspect. In fact, the definition of "folk" is something that "relates to the traditional art or culture of a community or region." So, folk witchcraft is, by definition, witchcraft that relates to a community. The practices would be familiar within the community or known via the community folk healer who performed for the village. Cultural witchcraft would be, in essence, the same because the practices are collectively utilized in that specific culture.

Many of these practices, though, are examples of closed practices, or off-limits to learn if you aren't from these regions or cultures. As discussed in chapter 1, cultural appropriation of practices is an issue in the witchcraft arena, and one not taken lightly. If certain rituals and practices stem from a culture that is not yours, it's best not to practice them. However, although the core fundamentals relating to these practices are universal, the terminology and specific spells or creations are closed. So, although this means that specific types of drums from a culture or specific rituals are "closed" from those not in the practice, you can still engage in the beating of drums or contacting the spiritual realm.

Consider how to integrate folk practices into your craft while still being respectful of the people who created them, despite the setbacks and oppression they experienced. Smoke cleansing is an excellent example of an off-limits ritual. It consists of a sacred rite of burning sacred herbs and resins in ceremonies practiced by Indigenous Peoples, which in their practice is referred to as "smudging," to cleanse and purify. Although the terms "smudging" and "smudge sticks" should be avoided, the idea of cleansing impurities from the body, mind, and energy has existed for centuries and can be embraced. Cleansing removes unwanted physical and mental debris and helps facilitate a relaxed state of mind for focus and intention setting. So, in place of these particular herbs, resins, and ceremonies, use fresh herbs such as thyme or mint for their cleansing abilities, and craft your cleansing ceremony to prepare the body and spirit for spells.

Regional Witches

Regional witches practice witchcraft related to the various geographical regions, such as Africa, the Americas, Asia, Europe, and the Middle East. Different areas around the world, historically, have their specific versions of witches and names for spirits and plants. These regions may have a distinct spiritual flare and unique magical rites, but as colonialism, settling, and diaspora occur over time, there has been movement and immersion of these practices to other places, creating subsets of practices all over. And because globalization has made access to other cultures easy, practitioners of all experience levels are more apt to delve into these other cultures and learn about additional tools and rituals to add to their witchy toolkit.

Here's where it can get tricky. When we think of regional witchcraft, we may think of practices that include specifics to that particular region. Homages to the mountains, symbolism, and uses of certain plants and animals from the area, names referring to deities and spirits that are isolated to that region and its beliefs. Bones of certain animals may be used in rituals in these areas and not in others, simply because those animals are not in that area. The specific practices are particular to the region. Regional witchcraft is a type of cultural witchcraft in that the practice is rooted in a very specific way of life for a certain group of people, and it often involves antiquated traditions. Regional witchcraft, and cultural witchcraft in general, refer to the customs that have existed, been molded, and changed in a region due to immigration, colonization, and societal change. And although many of the old customs are retained, some new additions (or subtractions) may also occur.

Heredity Practice Witches

Hereditary practice is a form of witchcraft that has been handed down through a single lineage. These practices are those that parents, grandparents, or other ancestors employed, passing on unique spells and rituals known to the family. Many types of witchcraft overlap this genre because many of the spells from among communities in certain regions, between cultures as immigration occurred, were passed down among family members. Appalachian folk magic is a great example (and just one example) of a hereditary practice and of how witchcraft overlaps. This practice contains influences from the Irish-Scots, Native Americans, and African Americans, all groups that made their way into the American Appalachian region, bringing with them the folk practices of their individual cultures and belief practices. These customs merged to create the spells and charms that grandmothers passed down to their children and grandchildren deep in the *hollers* of the mountains.

Folk Healers and Practitioners

Folk healers and practitioners come from traditions and cultures that use local herbal remedies, incantations, or suggestions to heal. These practitioners were also known as cunning folk, faith healers, traditional healers, medicine men and women, witch doctors, and granny or wise women. Although they arose from a variety of belief practices, from the Druids of the Celtic period and the "pellers" of 1800's Britain and beyond, we view these folk healers as sources of practical magic that alleviates illness, protects community, and offers countermagic against community witches wreaking havoc on livestock and the home. The folk healers could identify and draw out a witch, and this ability spanned practices—Southern American root doctors and Native American shamans alike could perform this duty, and a duty it was, for at the heart of the folk healer is community, and those healers played a central role in theirs.

Paganism and Modern Paganism

Paganism refers to practices incorporating pre-Christian practices and polytheism, or the belief in multiple deities. Paganism includes the Celtic, Greek, and Norse belief systems and the gods and goddesses comprising them—and that's just the tip of the pagan iceberg. After the Christianization of many regions, and the condemnation of their belief systems and those who held them, these systems morphed, were molded, or otherwise shamed into nonexistence to satisfy those in power. The Samhain practices observed by the Celtics, for instance, are a prime example of this molding. This fire festival was held as a way to contact the ancestors, honor higher beings, and take care of the provisions before the harshness of winter set in, but in an attempt to dismantle its pagan parts, Christianization morphed this festival into All Hallows' Eve (October 31), All Saints' or Hallows' Day (November 1), and All Souls' Day (November 2)—though, in our modern practice of Samhain, many still aim to keep the antiquated pre-Christian version alive. Harkening back to the archaic isn't just for pagan celebrations. It wasn't until the twentieth century that contemporary, or modern, movements began incorporating countless old pagan traditions and beliefs to create modern paganism, which incorporates a New Age spirituality, a reverence for nature, and an inclusive worldview. If that sounds broad, it is. Popular modern pagan practices include Druidry, heathenism, Thelema, and Wicca movements—to name a few.

Wiccan Witches

Wicca is a modern pagan religion created by Gerald Gardner in the middle of the twentieth century that draws from ancient pagan traditions and focuses on ritual practices. In its original format, it held a particular structure and hierarchy, and many still practice it in that structured sense, with witches moving up the spiritual ladder through rites and experience. Titles are emphasized in this structured version and many witches flourish in the community and its rigidity. However, many consider themselves Wiccan without adhering to these structures. There are many solitary Wiccan practitioners who honor both the god and goddess, a main tenet of Wiccan practices, and place reverence for nature as some of the most important parts of the practice. It can get a bit more nuanced from there. Although Wicca is duotheistic (honoring both a god and goddess), it certainly isn't unusual to see eclectic or broader Wicca practices ranging from polytheism to goddess monotheism. That's the beauty of the practice. One can take on a main identity, like "Wiccan," but then make it theirs. Wicca is often also practiced alongside witchcraft practices to incorporate deity.

Contemporary Witches

Contemporary witchcraft refers to practices that occur in the present, whereas eclectic witchcraft refers to practices created from a broad range of sources. Given these definitions, we can see how these two terms can be used to describe any of the previously described types of witches.

Let's revisit the Appalachian example. An Appalachian folk magic practitioner may call upon the learnings of their grandmother to help heal themselves, their family, their friends, and maybe others in the community. This practice alone draws upon regional and hereditary influences because the teachings were passed down from family members, and those practices were influenced by the immigration of different peoples and belief systems into the region. However, maybe when performing spells that incorporate railroad dirt, or involve a crossroads, where two sets of tracks intersect, the practitioner wants to call upon a deity for assistance, and this deity is from the Greek pantheon.

We see a melding of sources to create this practitioner's brand of magic. It is personal. In this scenario, eclectic, hereditary, and regional magic overlap. This could be considered contemporary witchcraft because it's a modern melding of practices. Contemporary witchcraft does not have to apply to a group of witches, and it doesn't require several people to practice it before it gets the title "contemporary." One person can practice their style of contemporary witchcraft, and others can practice their versions of contemporary witchcraft. There are no initiations, tests, or degrees associated with these types of practices unless you join a coven that might require them. Witchcraft is inclusive and free to all.

Folk and Traditional Witches

Folk and traditional witchcraft often incorporate a variety of contemporary forms of witchcraft, including folklore, spirit work, and ritual work and often animals, elemental beings, or fantastical creatures are involved. Rituals of varying degrees of difficulty often play a large role in these practices. Many witches who practice ceremonial or traditional witchcraft incorporate modern pagan practices while avoiding associations with Wicca. In this book, you'll find focused paths on these two types of witches (see chapter 3 on page 31).

Nature Witches

Nature witchcraft encompasses a large range of practices that can involve one or all of the elements. Within this category, you'll find all the elemental witches who practice water, green, and elemental magic, or healers who use a majority of ingredients from the elements, like ash, moss, soil, water, and so on. Elemental witches don't just use these items; often, reverence to the elements is part of the practice. Elemental witches give as much as they take, and they honor the elements in separate rituals or offer thanks.

An elemental witch's toolkit is most likely to include items from the elements, or the favored element of the witch. Hagstones, sea glass, water elixirs, moss, salt and sand, shells, driftwood wands, and so on would likely be utilized in the water witch's practice. For instance, but many times, elemental witches include ritual items from all elements in their practice, because each element has specific correspondences.

Elemental witches often also work with the elementals, or nature spirits, which inhabit the elements, such as the tree spirits, sylphs (air spirits), and undines (water spirits), though this is not always part of an elemental witch's practice. In this book, you'll find focused paths on elemental witches, with particular attention on green witches and water witches, as they are the most common elemental witches (see chapter 4 on page 57).

Hearth and Home Witches

Hearth and home witchcraft often incorporates pieces of cottage, hearth, hedge, and kitchen witchcraft. The hearth refers to a fireplace and the space around it and is associated with home and family. Historically, the hearth was the main source of heat in the home and its symbolic meaning still stands today. In magical practices, the hearth is seen as the hotbed of energy in the home and the place in the home that symbolizes safety, protection, blessings, abundance, and more. This is, perhaps, different from kitchen witchery, which utilizes food and drink to manifest intention and is generally centered in—you guessed it—the kitchen. Cottage witchery focuses on the kitchen and the hearth, but also lends itself to the garden, the bedstead, the windowsills, and the chimney, all those spaces where energy sits and can be used in magic (see chapter 5 on page 95).

Intuitive Witches

Intuitive witchcraft can incorporate a wide range of psychic abilities, divination, astrology, energy, and new practices. Intuitive witchcraft involves listening to oneself or the cosmos to gain insight on how to craft spells and rituals, to speak to spirits and ancestors for divination or guidance, and to guide the choice of tools, and for any clairvoyant purposes that don't involve deities or spirits on the other end.

Intuitive witchcraft often involves meditation or otherwise focusing the mind and body to be still enough to access that intuition. This seems easy, but it is actually difficult, and so intuitive witchcraft often involves a lot of practicing and observing, as well as logging events to hone skills and spot accuracies in your abilities. Whether meditative journeys to the spiritual realm or listening to a gut response when touching someone else's belongings, the intuitive witch trusts the messages that come through and allows those messages to guide spellwork and decisions made in everyday life. You'll find focused paths on the psychic, cosmic, and shadow witches, as they can encompass many of the other practices (see chapter 6 on page 119).

Eclectic and Niche Witches

Eclectic and niche witchcraft involves an endless list of unique and custom practices, specialized pathways unique to the practitioner. So, if you're not sure which type of practice is right for you, or you're looking to try something new, you might be interested in eclectic or niche witchcraft. Under this category, you'll likely find activist, art, crystals, fashion, glamor and beauty, tech, wellness, word, or other types of practices rooted in the present. In this book, you'll find focused paths on the crystal and wellness witches, as these are two of the most popular forms of eclectic practices you might see first that differ from the previous pathways (see chapter 7 on page 171).

PROMPTS FOR NAVIGATING THE TYPE OF WITCH YOU ARE

As we've seen, there are many types of witches and witchcraft, and many practices overlap, which allows you to get inspiration for your practice in a variety of ways. Use the journal prompts following to help you refine the path you want to learn more about. Take time to discover the type of witchcraft that calls to you deeply.

- What makes you feel at home or in your element? The sea, or the forest? What about a cozy fireplace? These spaces generally change the energy around you, making you calmer or more energized and inspired.

- When you envision your altar space, or the space where you'll do your spells and rituals and place your tools and ingredients, what do you see? Crystals or plants? Tarot and old grimoires? Sigils, candles, and more?

- Is there a practice or time period that feels like "home" to you, or safe, as though you are familiar with it? This may indicate which pantheon or culture interests you. It's okay to list several because these are likely the areas where your interests overlap.

- Do you feel drawn to higher beings, like elementals, deities, and working with the ancestors? What about humans? If so, which?

CHAPTER 3

FOLK & TRADITIONAL WITCHES

This chapter provides a brief overview of the contemporary forms of folk and traditional witchcraft and answers common questions many witches have. Folk and traditional witchcraft incorporate topics we often find in modern pagan practices, such as lore and legend, spirit work, ritual magic, and, oftentimes, animism. It's also practiced differently in various regions of the world because of its focus on community and culture. Both folk and traditional witchcraft practices incorporate simple magical tools, such as textiles, wax, string, plants, paper, and astrological events that can be seen with the naked eye. These practices focus on magic from simpler times, regardless of whether those practicing are from the Old or New Worlds. Old-World practices can sometimes be loosely defined as regions of the world before contact with the Americas but we'll dive deeper into the "Old World" and "New World" terms in the next section.

Folk witchcraft takes a mostly Old-World approach to witchcraft, from pre-modern perspectives. It looks to the magic from before the twentieth century, preserved from different regions or cultures. We often find folk witchcraft stemming from the hills of rural England or Scotland in the 1700 and 1800s. Because of this older approach, the witchcraft often includes items and approaches from that time: dipping candles for homemade tapers; utilizing kitchen twine for bundling herb; using garden plants for their healing properties; and so on. Folk witches also typically use the celestial bodies to guide their gardening and their magic.

Traditional witchcraft, on the other hand, focuses on where you are, not where you're from. Even with this focus, a witch may incorporate Old-World ways into their witchcraft because the region they're in likely uses artifacts from previous generations. Like folk witchcraft, traditional witch-craft asks you to seek magic in your backyard using local plants and the tools at your disposal. The craft can often take the form of a New-World approach to witchcraft because regions shift, change, and modernize over time.

Although you can practice traditional witchcraft wherever you *are*, you can also practice traditional witchcraft from a specific region that you're *not* from or currently living in. Many witches in the Western Hemisphere may, for instance, practice Slavic magic. Because of the internet and the ability to buy items online, anyone can be a part of a specific practice from far away. Again, be mindful of appropriation when approaching traditional methods from other cultures. Overall, these two practices move away from the religious-minded practice associated with Wicca. They don't ask you to adopt deities or any sort of structure to "move up" the spiritual ladder. There is no ladder. These traditions simply ask you to incor-porate the elements and tools available to you into your magic, with the culture of your chosen region sprinkled in.

Old World and New World

The term "New World" often refers either to the Americas or Western Hemisphere, whereas "Old World" is, generally, Africa, Asia, the Eastern Hemisphere, and Europe. The Western Hemisphere is home to North and South America and the surrounding waters that have boundaries of longitudes 20 degrees west and 160 degrees east. However, it's important to note that some geographers define the Western Hemisphere to be the half of Earth that's west of Greenwich, or prime meridian, continuing to the 180th meridian. This means the Western Hemisphere would include North and South America along with portions of Africa, Antarctica, Asia, and Europe. For Old- or New-World witchcraft practices, you can decide which division you'd like to work within for your practice. Consider doing research when you encounter new topics to broaden your knowledge.

A BRIEF HISTORY OF FOLK AND TRADITIONAL WITCHCRAFT

Traditional and folk witches often take an historical approach to the land wherever they are located. They might have old grimoires from the area, a collection of local lore and legends, and much of their practice can combine the connection between nature and history, though these aren't required to practice either traditional or folk magic. These witches may seek out spells, rituals, and recipes that come from a specific time, or they may incorporate old tales and folklore into their practice.

A witch may, for instance, place an offering to faeries in a home before its purchase, waiting for the faeries to nibble it as a form of their approval for the new homeowners to move in. This example is rooted in Old-World folklore, and other such possibilities are endless once you learn how to tap into resources for researching historical approaches to magic.

SYMPATHETIC AND CONTAGIOUS MAGIC

Spells from traditional or folk magic grimoires generally focus heavily on an archaic practice known as sympathetic magic. Sympathetic magic informs many of the Old-World and New-World magic techniques and includes two main tenets: the Law of Contagion and the Law of Similarity.

The Law of Contagion states that anything you've touched or that is on your person is imbued with your energy. For example, making bread with your hands to imbue your energy into it for an intended purpose. These items can then be used to represent or manipulate you, either in your magic or someone else's. The more saturated the item is, the better. So, many in the Old World used textiles stained with sweat or urine because it was thought they were packed with more of a person's energy. These items were often used in protection jars and in "deposits" (items buried in the home's chimney, mantle, or foundation for protection or blessing purposes) in Old-World homes. The New World would adopt this practice, evidenced by deposits in the homes of colonial America.

The Law of Similarity, on the other hand, says the cause will mimic the effect. For example, if you prick a poppet that symbolizes a person, that person will be pricked. Another aspect of the Law of Similarity is "like brings about like." If you suffer from an illness that creates a yellow coloring on your skin, your solution will involve a plant that causes yellow coloring, such as saffron. Those in the Old and New Worlds assumed their god made plants to look like the illnesses they treated, and, as you can imagine, this resulted in many mishaps in treatment.

ANIMISM IN FOLK AND TRADITIONAL WITCHCRAFT

A common theme among folk and traditional practices is the reverence for spirits and symbols, with many practicing magic using the elements of animism. The word *animism* is Latin for "anima," referring to breath, spirit, or life. Animism is the belief that all natural beings, including animals, plants, places, and even objects, hold a spiritual essence. When we call upon the cunning nature of the fox or the wisdom of the owl, or when we have a steer skull on our altar, our actions are often based on animism; these animals hold an essence we're trying to harness to manifest an intention in our magic.

When the ancient Celts donned animal skulls and danced, it was to infuse their minds with the essence of the animal. They wanted to, quite literally, get into the minds of that animal so they could hunt it better, and the skulls of the dead animal offered that ability because they still held the animal's spirit. Animism is a foundational element in the development of ancient human spirituality, and it can be identified in different forms throughout major modern world religions and cultures. Animism is a way of feeling and experiencing life, rooted in the respect for nature and life and the sentience of the living.

Focused Pathway 1
Traditional Witch

Traditional witchcraft focuses on the magic and lore of a certain region. This practice is an umbrella category known for combining witchcraft and folklore and that focuses on magic elements that came before Wicca and pre-modern times. Like many paths of the craft, traditional witchcraft includes spellwork, divination, and herbalism, and, for many, it may also incorporate honoring deities, saints, spirits, faeries, familiars, or ancestors.

GETTING STARTED (BEGINNER)

Because traditional witchcraft focuses on what's available locally, your practice will likely include those elements. And because these items are rich in history particular to your region, their meanings and uses may differ from how other witches use them. Horseshoes, for instance, have different specific uses depending on where you live. For example, coastal witches may use them to protect from sea-related disasters and sea spirits, whereas those in the hills may use them to protect their livestock from bewitchment. Traditional witches embrace the regional lore of their tools and use them for that purpose, even if popular books suggest other intentions. They understand there is nuance in magical artifacts that have existed for hundreds, or thousands, of years.

This section focuses on getting started in traditional witchcraft with the spirits of plants and familiars, as well as easy charms and textile magic. Following the introductory topics are more intermediate ones involving ancestry and otherworld spirit magic. When starting down a new path of witchcraft, it's important to note that each path is customizable to fit what's right for the practitioner. If you want to try a traditional witchcraft approach but don't want to incorporate one of the elements, you certainly can do it that way.

To craft an altar, we may include bits of old textile, glass, slate, or bottles found in our locale, photos of family or of the region, flora and fauna specific to your area or culture, deities that resonate with the culture, and any spiritual artifacts you have that have been passed down from friends, family, or ancestors. Because community is an integral part of this type of magic, the altar represents that communal quality.

Don't lose sight of yourself and your magic. In trying to accommodate your region and its culture, you may ignore what makes your particular craft special. Remember, these types of magic—folk, traditional, regional—wouldn't be what they are without the morphing of inclusions over time. You may carry the torch for this magic, but you're going to do what others have already done: change it a little to suit your needs. You're adding richness to the story. Find comfort in that.

Textiles and Charms

The use of textiles in traditional magic is strongly rooted, as they are often used as a form of sympathetic magic. More than that, they are used for braiding and binding and so they share with the universe the "who," via who possessed them, as well as the "what," via how we use them. In a more beginner-friendly way, they add color correspondence and they hold our other correspondences, like stones and herbs.

❧ Healing Sachet Charm

This charm is intended to encourage spiritual and emotional healing. The combination of herbs, stones, and symbols, when carried or placed under a pillow, eases the mind and spirit and allows for peaceful, restorative rest.

When to perform this spell:
Monday or Friday, at midnight, preferably when the moon is full or waning

Ingredients/tools:
Besom
Salt
Needle
Small, 2 x 4-inch (5 x 10-cm), muslin bag
Herbs: fresh lavender, lemon balm, marjoram, mint, verbena
Stones: blue lace agate, calcite of choice (pink for healing and love),
    desert rose selenite, or regular selenite
Purple thread

1. Clear your altar and sweep the besom over it to cleanse the space.
2. Place a circle of salt down for protection and place your needle, bag, herbs, and stones inside the circle.
3. Begin by threading the needle and enchanting it. As you hold it in your dominant hand, state, "As I thread, I imbue the healing; as I knot, I strengthen the feeling."
4. On the front of the bag, stitch a circle. Then, stitch a waning crescent moon (see page 142) within the circle. Within the crescent, stitch an equilateral triangle to represent the element of earth, the element of grounding and stability.
5. One by one, place the herbs in the bag. Then, one by one, mindfully add your stones to the bag. To stay in the moment and mindful, state out loud the names of the herbs or stones. This keeps the mind from wandering away from the spell.
6. When all the ingredients are in the bag, end the spell stating, "As I will it, it will be done."
7. Carry this sachet with you, place it on your altar, or lay it under your pillow to encourage healing and spiritual transformation.

INTERMEDIATE TRADITIONAL WITCHCRAFT

Intermediate traditional witchcraft moves beyond charms for healing and protection. A common feature of traditional witchcraft is contacting the ancestors for advice. In the times of the Celts, the Druids would contact the ancestors for guidance on keeping the community alive and well, and in many practices as far back as the Ice Age, designated community leaders (shamans) would venture to the spiritual realm, the otherworld, to contact the ancestors and other deities to seek guidance for the village. Today, solitary practitioners of all types of witchcraft make these journeys to ask for individual guidance.

Because these journeys require intensive visualization and the ability to "stay" in the meditation for an extended period of time, and because contact with spiritual entities is the goal, they are considered intermediate practices. As we can see from history, those who performed the journey were those appointed by the community as leaders who were spiritually able to access that realm. We can contact spiritual entities, be they deities, ancestors, and nature spirits such as faeries, in the earthen realm. But often, the way to reach them is to venture into the otherworld. This is a bit more dangerous because you're entering a place governed by different rules and inhabited by beings higher on the spiritual hierarchy than you. We leave when we feel it's time, and we always give gratitude for allowing us to journey there.

Ancestry Contact

When making contact with our ancestors, we may want to contact the ancestors of our chosen region to strengthen our bond, or we may want to contact our own ancestral lineage for personal guidance. Keep in mind: If working with a tradition that is not yours, be mindful not to appropriate cultural artifacts, as we talked about in previous chapters (see pages 16–17).

☙ Ancestral Scrying Spell

Following is a spell for contacting ancestors, be it of the region you've selected for your traditional witchcraft practice or of your ancestral lineage. These do not have to be the same.

When to perform this spell:
Monday or Sunday, at dusk or dawn

Ingredients/tools:
White pillar candle
Essential oil: sweetgrass, rosemary, or sage (see page 64)
Carrier oil of choice (see page 64)
Matches or a lighter
Rosemary bundle
Abalone shell or fire-safe dish
Tourmaline stone (placed on the altar for added protection
   or held as a necklace or in the pocket for protection)
Small dish
Large vessel to hold the small dish
Water to fill the bottom of the dish

1. Turn down the lights so barely any light is present.

2. Anoint your pillar candle with your chosen essential and carrier oil mixture.

3. Light your rosemary bundle and place it on the abalone shell.

4. Close your eyes. Breathe in and out while focusing on your breathing. Breathe in for 4 counts, and hold that breath for another 4 counts. Exhale for 4 counts. This is the 4-4-4 breath. As you continue to breathe, try to exhale an additional count, gradually working your way up to 7, if possible.

5. Hold up your hands, with your palms open, a little bit lower than shoulder height.

6.   Cast a circle of protection by stating out loud, "Around me goes a band of light; strong of will and filled with might. None comes in but those with ties; and when I will it, the connection dies."

7.   Light a match and use it to melt the bottom of the pillar candle. While the wax is soft, set the candle upright in the dish. The wax will solidify and "glue" the candle to the dish. Let the wax set.

8.   Place the dish with the candle into the larger vessel and add water to cover the bottom (but not to the brim). Light the candle.

9.   Perform the 4-4-4 breath again.

10.   State, "The water's the vessel for the ancestral divine. In flames and reflections, the messages hide. Show me your presence, if you will it so; as the elements collide, the messages show."

11.   Allow the flame to dance in the water's reflective surface, allowing your eyes to blur a little bit, while you inhale the rosemary smoke, breathing in for a 4-4-7 count. Look for any quick movements of the flame that indicate a presence. You may also feel this presence in the room.

12.   Movements of the flame, images in the reflections, or even messages intuitively placed in your mind may be messages from the ancestors. Look for imagery, letters, and numbers in the wax that's fallen. These are messages as well.

13.   When ready, end the session by stating, "I acknowledge the presence of ancestors conjured; I offer my gratitude for the messages sent. I end this connection to the ancestral ether; I close the door but maintain the tether."

Tools for the Traditional Witch

TOOL	DESCRIPTION	PROPERTIES
Bells	Bells are used in many religions and belief practices for spiritual cleansing and ushering in good spirits.	Bells are often used before any ritual to cleanse the space and they can be incorporated into spells to bring luck and increase prosperity.
Besom	Besoms are essentially small brooms. They were traditionally made of ash, birch, hazel, cranberry, and willow.	Besoms and brooms, no matter what they're made of, offer spiritual cleansing.
Bowls	These small clay or metal dishes are used for offerings and mixing ingredients.	Bowls allow us to connect spiritually to the elements and to a deity via offerings. Iron bowls offer protection; copper bowls offer healing; earthenware bowls connect us to the element of earth for grounding purposes.
Candles, beeswax	This environmentally friendly and natural wax is used to make candles that can purify the air.	Beeswax can offer guidance, insight, and messages about work, and help receive messages from the spirit world.
Candles, tallow	These candles, made from beef fat, were used from the Roman times until the 1500s. The tallow was then replaced with beeswax.	Tallow candles are an homage to the Old World, so they're used for ancestral connections. They're also infused with the essence of steer—resilience, strength, and protection.

Tools for the Traditional Witch *(continued)*

TOOL	DESCRIPTION	PROPERTIES
Cauldron	Generally made with cast iron, cauldrons allow witches to cook or mix ingredients for crafting magic over a heat source.	Cauldrons are used to blend and "cook" the magic, often crafting kitchen witchery by combining herbs and foods with specific intentions.
Fabric	Fabric and textiles are used to craft charms that carry their properties and they can be filled with other ingredients.	Fabrics, like cotton and felt, have properties of luck and protection whereas velvet, satin, lace, and silk have properties of wealth and love.
Incense	Incense comes in many forms: stick, cone, or loose. It's essentially a substance burned to produce a scent.	Incense properties depend on the herbs and resins used, but the main purpose is to connect to spiritual deities and provide an offering to them, or to induce meditative states.
Mirrors	Any reflective surface can be used as a mirror. Witches often paint mirrors black for scrying.	Mirrors are used in scrying magic, where the witch asks the mirror to show the future.
Needles or pins	Needles are used to stitch together poppets or to stitch symbols into bags and other textiles.	We can enchant the needle for a particular intention, and as we sew, we infuse the fabric with that intention. When placed in jars, they offer protection.
Sachets	These small drawstring bags are typically made of velvet or muslin.	Sachets are used to carry herbal blends and stones for charms.
Twine or string	This ancient fiber is used in crafts and for tools in knot or cord magic.	Twine or string is often used in binding, protection, and healing spells.

Focused Pathway 2
Folk Witch

Folk witchcraft has a heavy tie to the community and the culture of the region. These folk practices were understood by many in the village, and many were particular to the region based on the plants and herbs available. The practice may also include sigils that the community developed based on regional deities and beliefs, and ritual tools based on what was available in the region, like river water or coal.

At the heart of the folk practice is the folk practitioner, the appointed member of the community who was the source for practical magic: cursing, healing, and protective charms; poultices, teas, tinctures, and other healing methods; and incantations and various verbal charms passed down through generations. In the time of lack of modern medicine and the inability to access or pay for any medical practitioner, the folk practitioner was often accessed instead. Folk witches don't need to be skilled in herbal medicine to practice, nor do they have to be appointed by the community as the source of spiritual support. They simply practice the old ways of a region using what they have to do so.

GETTING STARTED (BEGINNER)

As we've shared, the folk path and the traditional path overlap a good deal. They are both steeped in the history and lore of a region and the culture therein, with folk witches taking a more Old-World approach to their magic rather than adopting contemporary shifts in the craft of the region. To begin the folk journey, witches may focus on elements and their magical components related to a particular region. Naturally, we think of plants and other inclusions of nature, and although that's certainly a part, other cultural elements may come into play in a folk witch's magic.

Spirits of Plants

Mystery and enchantment surround the natural world, holding close the imprints of time, changing through the seasons. Although connecting with the spirits of plants is not dedicated to any one tradition, many ingredients for spells and rituals come from plants and trees. Plants are accessible to most, regardless of location, and can recreate the techniques used in history and folklore.

Before you use plants in your practice, you should look at them through several lenses. Do a bit of research to see the rich history of the plant or tree in the chosen region and, perhaps, beyond. Go outside and compare the barks of trees or the leaves of sun plants versus shade plants. Look into the wildflowers and fungi of your chosen region. But keep in mind: Although we can learn much from other practitioners and books, touching a plant and working with it (growing it, harvesting it, tending to it) allows us to understand the plant so much more.

Many plants associated with traditional or folk practices are baneful, or poisonous, plants* known for their potency in spirit work. They are also associated with a practice called "the poison path," which focuses on the magical use of toxic and mind-altering plants. Because of their poisonous qualities, witches who use these plants are often at an advanced level.

*Safety Note: *Be sure to carefully study any type of plant you use, as it could be harmful and even poisonous to you or others. Allergic reactions are always a possibility, and many plants and herbs can be toxic at high doses. Research each carefully, wear gloves when handling, and always wash hands after use.*

Baneful, or poisonous, plants have, in large part, always been a part of the witchcraft scene, be it because of their appearance, how they're propagated, or their toxicity. In the Old World, plants were sometimes attributed to witchcraft because we didn't quite understand the plant. Mushrooms, for instance, earned their witchy lore because they seemed to propagate in circles out of nowhere; there were no roots to trace and they grew so quickly. Because of that lack of knowledge, those in the Old World attributed mushrooms' existence to the only other possible explanation: witchcraft.

The most popular baneful plant is belladonna†, the most toxic plant on earth, but there are more well-known baneful plants from the same plant family called nightshade, such as datura†, henbane†, and mandrake†. Other popular baneful plants include wormwood†, wolfsbane†, hemlock†, and foxglove†. Each of these plants is highly poisonous and has been used since antiquity for spiritual journeys and folklore practices. In fact, many of these plants were considered possible ingredients in the coveted flying ointments of lore, a hallucinogenic salve (apparently) used by witches to induce the mental state of flying.

†Safety Note: *We do not recommend nor advocate using any baneful, toxic, poisonous, or hallucinogenic plants or mushrooms.*

Baneful plants, however, can also act as familiars, which are teachers or guides into the otherworld. Plant familiars can help witches learn and grow in their practice. Witches will often select a plant to which they have a particular bond or spiritual closeness, and much like a familiar, the witch will tend to this plant a bit more closely. This plant serves as the witch's point of connection to the spiritual side, and so it may be placed on the altar when trying to connect to the spiritual realm in rituals, spells, and meditations, or worn around the neck. If the plant familiar is not baneful (like mint or thyme), it may be burned[‡].

[‡]**Safety Note:** *Never burn or ingest baneful herbs. Many of these plants might also cause skin irritation; always wear gloves when working with them*

❦ Celery Leaf Psychic Spell

Enhance your psychic abilities for spirit communication or dreamwork with the help of celery leaf, which mimics mugwort* and corresponds to its psychic powers based on sympathetic magic and the Law of Similarity (see page 34).

Safety Note: *Mugwort is an herb for enhancing psychic abilities used by many cultures for its mild hallucinatory effects. It is mainly used for astral projections, spiritual journeys, and trancework. It's related to wormwood, which also creates hallucinatory effects. In this book we do not recommend using these advanced witch herbs. This spell utilizes imagery. Creating a page in your Book of Shadows or grimoire, sketching different angles of the celery leaf, or printing a photograph, art print, or illustration allows you to study and connect with the spirit of the plant to use in spellwork.*

When to perform this spell:
Monday, Saturday, or any day, at midnight

Ingredients/tools:
Image of celery leaf
Matches or a lighter
Purple candle
Amethyst crystal
Journal or notebook

1. Clear and prepare a space for your spell.
2. Position the image of celery leaf in front of you.
3. Light the candle and visualize your intentions.
4. Gaze at the celery leaf image, studying the details of the plant.
5. Close your eyes and see the celery leaf in your mind's eye.
6. Hold the amethyst to your forehead and chant, "Open."
7. Meditate for 5 minutes, feeling your energy connect with the image of celery leaf in your mind and the crystal.
8. Note any images or symbols that appear in your mind during meditation, or any words or phrases that came immediately to mind. It may be helpful to write these down in a journal for later reflection.

INTERMEDIATE FOLK WITCHCRAFT

As with traditional witchcraft, the intermediate form of folk witchcraft often incorporates extended visualization in spells and rituals, accessing and working with familiars, fetches, and power animals. These acts of magic require strong foundational skills in visualization, which only come from practice. Following are some bits of this magic and how to practice it when you're ready.

Familiars, Fetches, and Power Animals

Familiars have been linked to witchcraft and other magical practices for centuries. The familiar was an animal or spirit that helped a witch connect to the spiritual realm. By "seeing through" the eyes of this animal, you could travel into the otherworld, the name often used for the spiritual realm, to speak to spirits. In times of antiquity, it was thought that the familiar was used as a way for the witch to travel undetected in the night, and the witch would use the animal to do their bidding, such as bewitch others. It was assumed that the familiar was given to the witch by the Devil himself, or otherwise inherited from a family member for magical purposes. Though a familiar could be any animal, the most common were hares and cats.

A familiar doesn't have to be a gateway to the otherworld or a tool at the witch's disposal; instead, witches today often have familiars that are simply spiritual companions that connect us to the natural world, or offer protection when performing magic. We may already know what kind of animal our familiar is, or we may have a pet that acts as that animal. If you don't know your familiar, reflect on dreams, meditations, or simple walks in the park. Are there certain animals that make themselves known to you? That animal may be a spiritual companion.

These animal or spirit connections are usually built on trust, and familiars often become assistants or companions. In archaic times, it was thought that the familiar stayed alive by sucking on the witch for sustenance, and often witchfinders would look for the suckling spot as evidence that someone was a witch. The witch also fed the familiar their blood as a means of connection. Although these forms of bonding with the familiar may not be practiced anymore, we did hold on to other methods of bonding: A witch cares for their familiar from birth and is very close to it, with the familiar almost acting like the witch's shadow.

Fetches, on the other hand, are known as a witch's double. They often appear during deep meditation journeys or out-of-body experiences, guiding and protecting the witch. Unlike familiars, which are actual tangible creatures separate from the witch, a fetch is a thought-form designed by the witch to roam around

Tools for the Folk Witch

In addition to the tools on pages 44–45, folk witches may also use these.

TOOL	DESCRIPTION	PROPERTIES
Animal horns, bones, or feathers	These are items from animals, such as bones, feathers, fur, nails, skulls, teeth, or symbols, which can be used to represent animal spirits. Note that some feathers, such as those from birds of prey, are illegal to collect without a permit. Be sure to research the laws in your region.	Different types of animal remains could be used to receive and hold offerings or serve as a home for the animal spirit.
Dirt	This is dirt taken from local places. Note that it is illegal to take dirt from private and public properties. Be sure to research the laws in your region.	Sprinkle dirt in your shoes or on your altar when performing spells.
Local herbs	A collection of herbs or herbal resources can assist with learning more about folk healing practices and practical magic.	Use to craft charms, poultices, teas, and tinctures for healing and protection magic.
Local waters	These are waters from a particular source, like a local river. Do not take waters from sacred wells or spaces, or any private property.	Depending on the kind of water you use, the intentions change. Use river water for spells related to transitions and change; lake water for divination spells; creek or brook water for cleansing spells; stump water (water found in old tree stumps) for spiritual connection and purification.

and do the witch's bidding. This fetch may, much like the familiar, roam into the otherworld or go outside to perform magic. And unlike the familiar, the witch can determine what the fetch looks like; it can appear as a witch's doppelganger, a different person altogether, or an animal spirit.

Power animals are a little different. Instead of being a representation of the witch, they are actually a spiritual guide(s). These power animals may come to you in the earthen realm, the dream realm, or in a meditative journey to share messages or offer comfort and guidance. Although you may have one of these animals as a pet, it is not the actual pet that's the power animal, as is with a familiar. Power animals are the animal in general: a rabbit, an owl, a horse. You could craft a fetch to *look* like your power animal, but when these animals show up in any realm, they are often carrying messages from the spiritual realm. What both familiars and fetches have in common is their purpose of performing magic, and what all have in common is the ability to strengthen the witch's connection to the spiritual realm.

✿ Spirit Connection Oil and Spell

Use this spell oil to help you connect with and spot your familiar. Although we may think we know what our familiar is, the familiar is not always what we want it to be, but rather an animal whose characteristics we need at a certain moment in our lives. The herbs suggested in this oil are best dried and ground. The longer you let the herbs steep in the oil, the stronger the oil can become. The ideal wait time can be 4 to 6 weeks for potency.

When to perform this spell:
Monday, Thursday, or Saturday between 7 p.m. and 9 p.m.

Ingredients/tools:
Pinch dried bay leaf
Pinch dried dandelion leaf
Pinch dried violets
Small (1- to 2-ounce) dropper bottle
1 to 2 ounces carrier oil, such as almond, jojoba, olive, or rosehip

1. Clear and prepare a space for your spell.

2. Drop a pinch of each herb into the dropper bottle

3. Fill the remaining space in the bottle with the carrier oil and seal the bottle.

4. Roll the bottle back and forth between your hands to warm the ingredients.

5. Close your eyes and focus on your intention for the familiar spirit connection.

6. Once you're ready to begin spirit contact, place a dot of oil on your forehead and sit in a comfortable position.

7. Relax your breathing and begin to meditate, feeling your energy connect with the oil.

8. Visualize yourself walking in a remote place—a forest, oceanside, or even a mountain.

9. See yourself and the place come to life and allow yourself to experience the sights, smells, sounds, and textures.

10. As you explore your remote place, be open to encountering a guide along the way. Chances are, a being you see could be your familiar guide.

11. If nothing arrives on your first try, keep trying and return often to get to know your familiar guide.

CHAPTER 4

NATURE WITCHES

Nature witches know the power and influence of the natural world. In this form of witchcraft, the witch uses the energies within one or all of the elements in spells and rituals. That energy is harnessed and kept, held and manipulated to bring about intention and change. After all, it's these elements that intertwine and collide to create the world around us. They produce that energy. The nature witch simply uses it. Nature witches work with all the elements and likely combine them, because all elements work together. Fire needs air to survive; earth needs water to turn seed into flower; and water tempers the flame. Because these elements rely on each other, it makes sense that, in nature witchcraft, magic relies on the symbolism of the elements and their pairings.

But like anyone, nature witches have favorites: a favorite element, a favorite season, and a favorite kind of energy to work with. And so, often, we see this kind of witch defined by five main categories: water witch, green (or earth) witch, elemental witch, air witch, and fire witch. And so, although nature witches do use all elements, water witches may work predominantly with sea oats and kelp, the lofty crag above the tide, and the traipsing of the moon, rather than tree spirits and faeries hidden in the hedgerow, which would be the domain of the green witch.

Because of this reliance on nature, it's common for the nature witch to live in tandem with the seasons—the reflectiveness and solitude of winter; the fertility and intensity of summer; and the transitional qualities of autumn and spring. Nature witches know these rhythms of change, and their magic takes advantage of the seasonal intentions by using that season's energy to bring about a witch's similar intentions, albeit on a smaller scale.

Nature witches also incorporate animism in their magic, as animism (see pages 34–35) speaks to the heart of this kind of nature witchcraft—that all natural items, plants, animals, objects, all kinds of things, hold a spirit, an essence. It is this spirit, this essence, that nature witches work with to bring about intention. A nature witch's focus on animism is, no doubt, inspired by the plants and critters around them, big and small. This, too, is often specific as to the "type" of nature witch someone is: Water witches may be inclined to work with sea beasts whereas the air witch may incorporate feathers or bird bones into their spells.

But we can't forget one of the most archaic inclusions in spiritual work that focuses on nature: astronomy. Since antiquity, humans have looked to celestial beings and honored them for what they give us: light, sustenance, life. These celestial beings play a role in a nature witch's practice, as the moon phases influence the intentions of our magic and the sun is still honored in rituals and sabbats. The planets, too, hold essence, energy, and intention, and we can harness them, too, if we wish (see chapter 6 for more on the sun, moon, and planets and their influences). Following is a more in-depth discussion of using nature in your practice and focuses on the specific types of nature witchery that may appeal to you. Don't feel as though you have to pick just one element; combining them allows you to get specific about intentions to manifest exactly what you need.

WORKING WITH NATURE

But how does a witch "use" or "work with" nature? The answer is a trusty vague response: It depends. Witches are still inventing spells that incorporate the elements in really interesting ways. The tried-and-true method is to utilize flora, fauna, and items from the elements in spells. This may mean sprinkling dried kelp or seaweed across thresholds to bring about prosperity or hanging fisher floats outside the home to promote protection.

One of the other main ways to work with nature is through symbolism. Animals, plants, celestial bodies—nearly any of these we imagine can be symbols for larger concepts. Just what they symbolize likely depends on the culture and time period, and so you may want to do a little research depending on your interests. We may wear the imagery of an animal that symbolizes courage, plant some herbs that symbolize safety or happiness, or inscribe phases of the moon in candles to symbolize the meaning of each phase (more on that in a bit). We may carry bones or feathers of the owl to encourage wisdom, or use the owl feather to inscribe the word "wisdom" in a white candle, for instance.

As you can see, there are many ways to "use" natural items in spellwork. It just comes down to what feels natural, what our intuition tells us to do as well as the traits of the element at hand. Anyone who knows their astrological sign can tell you the traits they inherited from the stars, and this is, in part, rooted in which element your sign is under, and you can choose an element depending on the kind of magic you want to do:

△ The air element rules over mental clarity, communication, inspiration, creativity, children's magic, wisdom, and intellectual pursuits. Gemini, Libra, and Aquarius are air signs.

▽ The earth element favors rationality and objectivity, grounding and practicality, and the signs Taurus, Virgo, and Capricorn are earth signs.

▽ The water element favors emotion and intuition above pragmatism. Water also houses the dream state and unconscious desires. Cancer, Scorpio, and Pisces are water signs.

△ The fire element governs passion and drive, and is often related to spheres of life where assertiveness, aggressiveness, bravery, and strength are needed, like business. It also relates to intensity and romantic pursuits, often dealing with sex and initiation of relationships. The fire element is considered the more unstable of the elements because of its intensity. Aries, Leo, and Sagittarius are fire signs.

And so we can begin to see each kind of nature witch take shape. Green witches honor and appreciate the natural world, using trees, rocks, plants, herbs, essential oils, crystals, and botanicals. Water or sea witches harness the energy of water, using fresh or saltwater in spells for scrying, bath magic, weather, or working with one's emotions. Water witches often live near bodies of water and use sand, shells, or nautical-inspired items in their craft. Air witches focus on using tools related to the air, such as wands, wind and wind chimes, feathers or birds, cleansing smoke or incense, and other air charms. The invisible element of air allows witches to focus on the mind and communication spells. Fire witches use the element of fire in their practice. Candles, burning magic, bonfires, solar magic, or symbols representing fire are all options. And although each element is vastly different, each holds symbols for the same thing. For instance, in stability spells, a water witch may use sand, a green witch may use salt or dirt, a fire witch may use ash, and an air witch may use nest twigs. Each item has the same goal: To bring about stability. Finally, elemental witches use the four elements and their symbolic correspondences to bring about intention.

Because the nature witch may also focus on seasons, the inclusions in spellwork may shift based on what's seasonally available in the region. Although imports and online shopping can support the nature witch who is limited in what's available locally, many nature witches use the shifting of the seasons to "freshen" their magic and bring in new symbolism. Spring's little rabbits may be rife with fertility symbolism, but in autumn, the rabbit (or hare, though these are a bit different) align more with spiritual journeys, as it's one of the animals known for its status as a familiar (see page 51). Likewise, the cleansing qualities of thyme and mint in spring will, in winter, be replaced by the purity of white birch.

For timing spells, the nature witch likely turns to moon phases and the relationship between the sun and the planets. The moon can add energy to spells by way of its current phase. The *waxing moon* corresponds to rebirth, hope, courage, bravery, and any spell that "adds" something to our lives, like luck, love, or money. In this phase, the moon is "growing" in size, and so our magic mimics that, often focusing on spells for growth. The *full moon* symbolizes power and fertility. In this phase, the moon has reached its peak in terms of emotion. If you want to perform a bravery spell, the full moon promises bravery at its strongest. If you want cleansing, not a speck of negativity would be left behind. The full moon has optimum power and control, so no matter the spell's intention, the full moon will manifest it as much as possible. The *waning phase* relates to "subtractive" spells that remove something from our lives. We may use this phase in spells related to breaking habits, ending relationships, letting go of old feelings, and spiritual cleansing. The waning phase is also for transformation, endings, change, and wisdom.

The sun and its relationship to the planets can help us choose a certain time of day to perform magic. This is a complex practice wherein may scholars have devoted their time and love for astronomy and astrology to identify the most optimum times of day for a broad range of spellwork and is beyond the scope of this chapter.

A Brief History of Nature Magic

Living in tandem with nature is quite literally one of the fundamental experiences of humans. From the nomads of the Ice Age to the settlers new to land in any given time or culture, humans have had to live in tandem with the seasons and celestial bodies, basing their forages and hunts on time of day, seasonal impact, and so on. Their lives depended on it. However, around ten thousand years ago in various parts of the world, we saw the emergence of agriculture, including animal agriculture, which meant people could stay in one spot and cultivate sustenance. Domesticating animals, planting seeds to grow crops in fields—these were significant, life-altering developments. And while cultivation didn't remove the hunting and foraging aspects of life, it certainly changed how we perceived the gathering of foods. Humans still had to live in tandem with the seasons and their locales regardless of agricultural changes, a fact true today, even with globalization.

The *Old Farmer's Almanac* is a testament to this relationship between humans and agriculture and a reliance on season and region. The *Old Farmer's Almanac* emerged in 1792 as the source for information on sowing and gardening, harvesting, weather predictions, sunrises and sunsets, and more. It also contained astrological information, such as the best moon phases for harvesting plants. But it certainly wasn't the first of its kind. The average colonial American woman would have gathered from Daniel Leeds' almanac (1687) the best time to harvest her herbs (yes, her) based on planetary influence. The almanac's astrological inclusions were met with a bit of contention, and this contention strengthened over time and influenced the approach to occult inclusions in almanacs.

Nature magic also comes from early cultures and their desire to rationalize the natural phenomena they witnessed. Without scientific understanding to make sense of the world around them, cultures relied on shared interpretation of what must be going on, and so crafted beings that controlled various bits of the world, each with their particular interests and personalities, each guardians of some facet of nature. Often, these beings existed in tales meant to guide the fallible human through life, but they were also intended to explain the way things in the natural world came into being. Be it Celtic, Greek, Incan, Japanese, Mesopotamian, Native American, Zulu, or countless others, mythology offered what limited human understanding could not: an answer. Deities, because they are often rulers of celestial bodies and nature, are still a part of the nature witch experience, but not every nature witch includes them in their practice.

Unique Aspects of Nature Witches

While all witches can tap into the energy inside them and around them to add to their magic, it's the nature witch who does this with full force. This witch has a strong relationship with the elements, and when energy is what fuels the magic, the ability to pull in this elemental energy with ease may set the nature witch apart. Beginner witches, in general, may have an easier time working with nature magic, because beginner witches may not know quite how to find and build energy inside themselves, or be able to conjure that energy easily. The elements can support this witch, guiding like a parental figure. Nature witches also do not have to rely on research and tales of their region or culture for instruction on how to perform magic as traditional or folk witches might. The universal quality of nature and its inclusions allow for freedom from any feelings of needing to "get it right" or be "historically accurate."

Why Green Magic and Water Magic Are Popular

Fire and air are important, and they control our lives. The bonfires lit at Celtic Samhain celebrations to honor the sun are a testament to that fact. We have understood that these elements, too, are a requirement for life. However, in the magical realm, we often see more green witches and water witches rather than air and fire witches. Why? We may never know the exact reasons witches play favorites here, but we can surmise that air and fire witchery relies on the fickle, sometimes absent, bits of nature—the transparency of air and the disappearance of smoke. The inevitable end of the candle flame once the wax is burned hrough. A match has a quick life and, soon enough, the flame goes out. Although we can always create new flame, breath, and smoke, these elements exist in their temporariness.

There is permanency in green and water witchery. Earth is always present, ready to be explored and honored, and we know we can always seek it out when in need of the energy of a plant or tree. The same is true for water. The stream will be there tomorrow, just as it is today. In essence, the permanency of these elements may be what makes them more popular. They're easier to access.

The spiritual connection of water may also be alluring. Sacred wells, rivers connected to the otherworld, the rushing sounds of water said to be the indicator of a shamanic journey, holy waters. These all hold a distinct spiritual quality. And although all elements are spiritual, perhaps, water may be considered "more" spiritual than fire and air. This hierarchy may include the earth as well because Mother Earth is held particularly sacred in many cultures, no matter her name.

Tools for the Nature Witch

TOOL	DESCRIPTION	PROPERTIES
Apothecary bottles	Nature witches who want to incorporate a traditional component may use old apothecary jars to adorn their altars and hold their herbs.	The color of apothecary jars or old jars, in general, can add correspondence. No matter the jar, it should always be cleaned and thoroughly dried so moisture doesn't affect any items in the jar.
Candles	Chime candles or pillar candles are easily available and relatively inexpensive. They add color correspondence to magic. Candles appeal to the fire, earth, and air elements.	Use chime candles for spells, as they burn down quickly, and many spells, typically, call for candles to "burn through."
Crystals	Crystals are remnants of earth, so the nature witch may venture over to the eclectic witch's realm to have crystals on the altar.	Crystals offer individual correspondences, but they all relate to stability and foundation, properties governed by the earth element.
Dried flowers	Common flowers used in magic include calendula or marigold, coneflowers (echinacea), daisies, dandelion, and jasmine.	Dried flowers are great to adorn altars and provide offerings to deities. Like herbs, they infuse space with individual intentions.
Essential oils and carrier oils	Essential oils* come from the plant after distillation of the plant material. They don't contain any of the organic material, but they have the properties of the plant in the oil. There are countless types of essential oils from plants. Essential oils incorporate the earth and water elements. Carrier oils are base oils that are used to dilute essential oils when applying to the skin or when essential oils are being handled, as essential oils can be potent and cause allergic reactions, burns, and be toxic in high dosages. Common carrier oils are coconut, jojoba, apricot kernel, sweet almond, olive, rosehip, grape seed, and argan.	Blend essential* and carrier* oils into mixtures to anoint candles in spells or add to loose incense and bath salts to provide a specific intention. When diluting essential oils with a carrier oil, it's important to follow each oil's guidelines for dilution. As a general guideline for adults, add 15 drops essential oil per 6 teaspoons carrier oil for a 2.5 percent dilution. For a 3 percent dilution, add 20 drops essential oil per 6 teaspoons carrier oil. For children, add 3 to 6 drops essential oil per 6 teaspoons carrier oil for a 0.5 to 1 percent dilution. ***Safety Note:** *Carefully read and follow the manufacturing directions and recommended dilution ratios for both types of oils, as well as for any potential allergic or toxic reactions.*

Tools for the Nature Witch *(continued)*

TOOL	DESCRIPTION	PROPERTIES
Feathers	Feathers are part of the air element and the earth element, and the bird they belong to will influence their correspondences. Note that some feathers, such as those from birds of prey, are illegal to collect without a permit. Be sure to research the laws in your region.	Generally, feathers usher in change and good energy, and they move and direct energy, often to remove it. The corresponding bird will add intention to the space upon cleansing.
Herbs	Common herbs† for the nature witch include lavender, mint, rosemary, sage, and thyme. These are easily grown and widely available. Herbs correspond to the earth element. †**Safety Note:** *Exercise caution with all herbs, as allergic reactions are always a possibility, and many herbs can be toxic at high doses. Research each herb carefully, wear gloves when handling, and always wash hands after use.*	Use these herbs by braiding them (rosemary and lavender) together, burning them after they're dried, or simply growing them, which fosters their intentions in the space they inhabit.
Incense	Incense (cones, loose, or sticks), like candles, combines the earth, fire, and air elements.	There are many herbal blends‡ for specific intentions. ‡**Safety Note:** *The toxicity of the smoke of certain plants should always be considered when crafting an incense blend.*
Matches	Matches offer a combination of the fire and air elements, and we can incorporate the woods they're made from into our magic for added correspondence.	Matches are ideal for the traditional nature witch who wants a more "primeval" way to add these elements into their magic. Matches are generally made of pine, which symbolizes protection.
Shells	We often incorporate shells on altars as a "dish" to hold herb bundles and loose herbs. They appeal to the earth element.	Different shells have different intentions, but they all offer protection and stability, an homage to their purpose in the sea— protecting the animal inside.

Focused Pathway 3
Green Witch

As we discussed briefly, green witches focus on the earth element. These witches are also sometimes gardeners, herbalists, and foragers and may work with creatures or the fae. Green witches are often drawn to the healing arts and might enjoy crafting healing herbal teas, tinctures, or natural products, like balms and salves infused with herbs and essential oils. In this, we see the overlap of the green witch and the folk witch.

GETTING STARTED (BEGINNER)

For the green witch, the magic comes from understanding the green world, so a great place for the green witch to start is to become familiar with the earth and with common witchy plants. If you're not a gardener, begin with an easy-to-grow plant, like mint. Start by drawing a circle deosil (clockwise) into its soil to encourage growth and "abundance" in the harvest. You can also incorporate other symbols into the soil, like a heart for love or a waxing crescent moon for growth, by watering the plant with a watering can with a thin spout. In this, we develop our connection with the green world and with the plant, in particular.

The next step when working with the green world might be to dry and jar your herbs and plants. Many green witches have herbs and plants hanging upside down in airy, dark, cool spaces so they may use them in recipes, teas, and healing ointments as well as floor potpourri (flowers scattered on the floor to offer intention and cleansing, a throwback to more traditional times). Others simply enjoy having the herbs hanging to encourage the intentions in the space they occupy.

We may also craft braids out of vine plants, such as ivy, grasses, and long tendrils of lavender and rosemary, and place these around the home to build power; as we braid, we add our energy to the plants to create a braid of concentrated energy, to be released in a spell whenever we wish. Braids can also "bind" energies, and so we can craft "worry" braids of mallow (another vine plant) and thyme, infusing the braid with all our anxieties, thereby getting it out of ourselves.

❧ The Garden Witch's Wreath

One way to work with green magic is to craft wreaths, which have protective energies and can infuse the space with the qualities of the herbs and plants they're made of. These wreaths are placed on the front door to act as a guard against those who may wish ill will, or to mark the space as sacred or spiritual. You may not look at your seasonal wreath the same again!

When to perform this spell:

Sunday or Thursday, any time

Ingredients/tools:

Dried plants and greenery, such as lavender fronds, dried cedar or
  pine fronds, and coneflowers
Wreath base, such as a ready-made grapevine wreath
Glue gun
Glue sticks
Any textile or ribbon of choice, preferably in greens and purples

1. Begin by plotting where you want your plants and greenery to go on the wreath base. Consider layering them out and allowing the coneflowers to take precedence as the focal point. Coneflowers symbolize wisdom and health, prime properties we aim for in the home. You may wish to remove and save the dried petals on one side of the flower heads, as these will likely crumble when placed up against the wreath base.

2. When you have your layout determined, glue the fronds in hidden areas, focusing on the layering of intention. All inclusions here correspond to protection, healing, and cleansing, and their colors lend a healing and spiritual connection.

3. When done, wrap your textiles (if chosen) around the wreath, beginning with the right-hand side and moving deosil (clockwise). Then, add 9 knots. As you tie each knot, state one of the following lines:

    "A knot for cleansing."
    "A knot for protection."
    "A knot for healing."
    "A knot for psychic awareness."
    "One for spirituality."
    "One for abundance."

"Another for safety."
"The eighth to build power."
"The ninth to seal it."

4.   Hang the wreath on the front door or above a fireplace or altar.

INTERMEDIATE GREEN WITCHCRAFT

Intermediate green witches may wish to move beyond plant correspondences, moon phases, and symbolism in their magic and look toward bones, stones, and sticks as divinatory tools. They may invite faeries into their homes to strengthen spellwork, provide blessings, or even help with housework. And they may wish to strengthen their relationship with the elements by way of working with the elementals (or the spiritual beings in charge of governing the elements). This is different from working with the elements, which is bringing their symbolism into our magic. Instead, we're working with spiritual beings.

Intermediate Skills: Working with the Elementals

The elementals are spiritual entities that create and protect the elements, and there are different types for each element: the undines (water), the gnomes (earth), the salamanders (fire), and the sylphs (air). Each group has its particular proclivities, but what you need to know about them is that they aren't quite like faeries or deities in that they have human-like judgments and tempers. Rather, they are energies that move about and perform duties.

The elementals do have qualities, though, and too much of an element in your spellwork can cause more harm than good. Undines, for instance, are great for tapping into our intuitive self, but they guide our emotions as well, and too much undine focus can lead to emotional upheavals and an inability to see truth through feelings. Gnomes encourage rational thinking and stability, but that can lead us to lack hope and creativity. Salamanders aid us in passion and motivation, but they are volatile and highly energetic, leading to misguided energy. And, sylphs craft the winds and encourage inspiration, mental clarity, and creativity. But too much sylph influence can cause a lack of rationality and objectivity. As in life, the elements are great in moderation, and so the intermediate witch calls upon the elementals as spiritual entities that can guide and support.

❧ Spell to Ask the Earth Elementals for Support

For this spell, we craft ink and channel the earth elementals before the actual spell we want to do. This asks for their support and their presence for the spell. Earth elementals offer stability and rational guidance, so they are best for spells concerning emotions and change.

When to perform this spell:
Tuesday, any time (6 p.m. is ideal)

Ingredients/tools:
Small pot
Black walnuts, semi-shelled or semi-crushed (to enable
   the inside of the walnuts to be released when boiled)
1 cup (240 ml) vinegar
Fine-mesh sieve
Glass jar or ink well
Salt
Green chime candle
White chime candle
Brown chime candle
Piece of paper
Bamboo skewer, quill with a metal nib, or some other writing tool
An offering, such as moss, dried aster flowers, or sweetgrass in a small dish

To make the ink:

1. In a small pot, combine the black walnuts and vinegar and simmer over low heat until a strong brown-black color emerges, about 30 minutes.

2. Using gloves, strain and decant into a glass jar or ink well.

For the spell:

1. Craft a circle of salt.

2. Along the salt circle, in an equidistant triangle with the point facing downward, arrange your candles.

3. Using salt, draw a horizontal line through that triangle, closer to the point of the triangle than the middle. This is the symbol for the earth element (see page 59).

4. On your paper, using your writing tool and your ink, inscribe the intention of the spell you wish to perform after this elemental invocation spell. Use words such as love, foundation, grounding, friendship, healing, and so on.

5. Place the paper in the smoke of each candle, and as you do, state, "The power isn't mine alone; earth elementals, I conjure you home. Please assist me in my magic." Then, place the paper in the center of the triangle.

6. Keep the same setup while you perform your other spell. You will likely feel a presence as you do it.

7. After the spell, place the offering dish in the middle of the triangle and share a heartfelt "thank-you" to the elementals. Close the circle by stating that the spiritual opening is closed and no entities can now cross through. Allow the candles to burn out.

8. Leave this setup overnight. In the morning, place the offerings in the garden or near the front door, along with the salt you used.

Focused Pathway 4
Water Witch

The water witch works with all types of water, water elementals and entities, and wet locales in their magic. Often, the water witch's focus is to build spirituality, psychic awareness, intuition, and feminine wisdom. The water witch may also work with the moon as the moon impacts water and its intensities. They may focus on dreams and other subconscious work and incorporate meditation, sleep, and spiritual journeys into their practice.

Waters collected have different powers depending on their source. Marsh and bog waters offer reflection and shadow work powers, whereas tumbled spring and small creek waters offer peace and beginnings. Sea water offers protection and clarity, as well as a spiritual or ancestral connection, whereas river waters are for removals or cleansing. Witches may collect different types of waters to use in their magic, from anointing candles and charging stones to blessing their tools. Lake waters or fairy pools offer a glimpse into the otherworld and into ourselves, and so use these waters for scrying.

Water witches may expand upon this focus to include watery animals and their symbolism. Dolphins, turtles, sea urchins, whales, sharks, and so on all have different intentions, and so their symbolism is often worn or otherwise used in the water witch's spells. Water animals, such as turtles, sea urchins, and whales, often symbolize protection. Water plants, like animals, may be utilized—kelp and sea oats offer abundance and prosperity. Water witches can use waters to charge stones and stones to charge waters because the energy transfer works both ways. You might place a rose quartz into spring water and place it under the waxing moon to charge that water for self-love rituals, or you may place a smoky quartz in river or sea water to cleanse it of negative energies.

GETTING STARTED (BEGINNER)

The water witch might begin by collecting different waters and placing them in containers for different uses, such as in roll-ons to anoint the body, in dropper bottles to anoint items and candles, and in spray bottles to adorn the air with the intention of the water. To these waters we can add crystals and oils to build intention (see more on crystals in chapter 7).

The beginner water witch may not be concerned with the different types of waters and their correspondences just yet. Those are nuances of magic that we focus on as we move into intermediate work. Rather, beginners focus on the broad correspondence between water and emotions, and how water causes emotions to ebb and flow much like the element does.

❧ Uplifting Floral Water Spray

Floral waters are an excellent way to infuse botanicals to create intentional, spelled waters that can be used to cleanse your area or uplift your emotions. The best water for floral waters is either spring or distilled to allow the properties of the flowers to thrive. Try flowers with a pleasant fragrance, such as rose, peony, lavender, jasmine, or gardenia, for this floral water spray. If foraging your flowers, make sure to research about foraging in your local area. Add essential oils, crystal chips, or salt to customize further and empower your spelled floral water.

When to perform this spell:
Monday or Friday, any time (midnight is ideal)

Ingredients/tools:
3 or 4 fresh flower heads or petals, from a reputable source or your garden
Glass jar with lid
Spring or distilled water
Fine-mesh sieve
Spray bottle

1. Cleanse your materials, if needed.

2. Place the flower heads or petals in the glass jar and top with the water. Seal the jar and let stand to infuse for a few hours, or up to 24 hours.

3. Roll the jar in your hands and state your intention.

4. Drain the mixture and decant it into a spray bottle. Your spray is now ready to be used.

5. Combine your intention as you spray your floral water.

INTERMEDIATE WATER WITCHCRAFT

Intermediate water witches may work more with the relationship between water and the other elements. The elements work in tandem, so when we move beyond the basics of nature magic, we begin to use the relationships among the elements as symbols in our magic. For instance, if we want to temper our emotions with rationality and encourage objectivity, we may couple water magic with green magic. If we need a bit of motivation to start anew and see things differently, we may pair water and air together. And if we need a bit of spark or passion in our relationships, fire and water may be the pairing to use.

Intermediate water witches may also begin strengthening relationships with water elementals, and call upon them for support in their spells. Because all elements have elementals, the water element is no different, and these beings help you strengthen your intuition and tap into your emotions to learn more about yourself.

Scrying may be another avenue for the water witch. In scrying, we gather a dish of waters charged with spiritual heightening stones, such as quartz, moonstone, and amethyst, and set it under the full moon's light, with a candle placed nearby so the flame is reflected in the water, and with a circle of salt cast around it for protection. An incantation is then whispered to ask the spiritual side to come through and share messages via symbols and imagery. Such activities require a honed spiritual connection. Intermediate witches may meditate or place themselves in a trance using drum music and swaying the body before scrying to help with their visualizations.

Intermediate witches may also delve into the rich water or sea folklore of a certain region or time period and incorporate the charms and incantations they read about in their magic. This may include spells for tempering storms or bringing about rain, charms for keeping ships safe at sea or protecting sea-bound witches from dangerous travels and ill-wishing sprites, or knot spells for encouraging favorable winds and soothing the lightning.

Weather magic may also appeal to the intermediate water witch as weather magic moves beyond using the element(s) at your disposal and ventures toward being able to control or influence those elements. That kind of magic takes special skill because it requires a relationship with the elementals that govern weather.

Tools for the Water Witch

In addition to the tools on pages 64–65, water witches may also use these.

TOOL	PROPERTIES
Animal imagery	Sea animals all have different correspondences. Add their imagery to altars and sigils to encourage their intentions. Some witches adorn their spaces with animal bones.
Fisher floats	Fisher floats are glass bubbles attached to nets used for protection and guidance.
Hagstones	Hagstones are stones that have a hole worn in them from repeated interaction with water; the water has, over time, created a crater and softened the edges. These powerful stones offer protection and spiritual connection.
Sand	For the water witch, sand accompanies salt as a protective tool. Sand can also be used for stability and grounding spells, as well as spells related to banishing or burying something.
Sea glass	Sea glass comes in a variety of colors that can add correspondence to your magic, from greens and blues to rich purples, whites, and browns. Reds and oranges are less common. Use these in growth and transformation spells.
The moon	The moon affects the tides, and so its connection to water magic is undeniable. Use the moon and its reflection in waters to add power to that water, or simply perform your spells during a certain moon phase.
Waters	Waters can be used as simple offerings, but, generally, use waters to charge and cleanse gemstones, anoint candles with the intentions of the specific kind of water, and scry for spiritual messages.

Weather Magic

What kind of weather magic you do depends on your elemental interests. Here, we'll focus on water weather magic, but keep in mind you could ask for winds to move seeds in the air or bring about change, encourage the clouds to venture onward so the sun's warmth coats the plants, and so on. One of the most common bits of water weather magic done is to impact rain. This could be to encourage rain for cleansing or strong harvests, or to halt storms to protect ships or ease the worries of children afraid of lightning. The uses are unlimited. In the next spell, we combine the water and earth elements by using water with heather blossoms and a grapevine, all of which have a connection to water and rainmaking.

❧ Rain Spell

To encourage soft, cleansing rains, we can appeal to the water elementals, the undines who control the rains, and so we ask for their assistance. We can then collect any rainfall to use in future spells for beginnings, gentle change, transitions, and hope, or we can perform cleansing spells during that rain. Be mindful: Do not perform weather spells just to prove your power or see what you are capable of. Elementals, and spiritual entities, in general, don't take kindly to witches using them for ego boosts. Communicate and ask for assistance when you need it, and always have an offering and a hearty thanks on hand.

When to perform this spell:
Monday, any time (10 p.m. is ideal)

Ingredients/tools:
Small muslin sachet filled with dried heather flowers
One 12-inch (30-cm)-long dried grapevine or rose stem
3 long fern* fronds

1. Position yourself near a tumbling brook or tiny waterway, such as a stream, with your materials close by.

2. Place the muslin sachet in your nondominant hand for ease later in the spell.

3. Using your grapevine or rose stem, begin churning the water to "reroute" its movement deosil (clockwise) circle. Allow this to become more intense as you envision rain clouds venturing inward and a drizzle beginning. As you continue to "churn" the water, charm it by whispering, "Water sprites that live within, we move the waters and rain begins. Upon your will, the clouds upend, and the earth feels raindrops on its skin." Repeat this to build power.

4. As you continue this movement with your dominant hand, sprinkle the heather blossoms from the sachet within the circle you're drawing in the water with your grapevine or rose stem. Continue your visualizations and your incantation until you feel a sense of ease and completion.

5. Place the fronds in the water to seal the spell and as an offering to the water sprites.

*Safety Note: *Some species of ferns can be toxic.*

Focused Pathway 5
Elemental Witch

Elemental witchcraft is focused on the symbolism and roles that the elements play in our lives, and how we can work with those to bring about intention. As we discussed earlier in this chapter, each element has its own correspondences or traits that it governs. So we can do two things when we want to perform elemental magic:

1. We can use the elements as symbols in our magic to represent our intentions. We can use a candle and its flame to represent the passion within ourselves, for instance, or a dish of salt to represent stability and grounding if that is what we are calling in our spell.

2. We can ask the elementals, the spiritual beings that govern the elements, to assist us in our magic (see page 71). This is, just like green witchcraft, intermediate work.

Some cultures and practices add wood, ice, and metal as additional elements that influence us and the energy around us. Elemental witches widen their practices beyond green (earth) magic and water witchery to incorporate these additions, and they focus on the relationships between these elements, as well as the roles the elements play in the wild, as symbols and metaphors in their spellwork. Ice may freeze the pond, for instance, halting movement, but it doesn't kill the animals underneath. The elemental witch may use this symbolism to reference a bit of healing and happiness underneath a bout of stagnancy in their lives.

The elemental witch may also pay particular attention to alchemy, a philosophy that focuses on the transformation and change, notably on the chemical or reactionary level as it relates to metals. Alchemists wanted to, among other goals, transform base metals (like copper) into silver into gold. Alchemy mainly focuses on changes on the chemical level that lead to large, overarching shifts—little happenings that result in large-scale alterations.

Considering these little changes, the elemental witch may look at how elements cause change within each other, such as fire melting ice into water or water causing rust in metal, and will use these interactions as symbols for the elements within, for example the emotionality of water, the passion of fire, the motivation and intellect of air, and the rationality of earth. If witches want to temper their

passions with a bit of groundedness, they may use the elements of fire and earth in spells to bring it about.

The elemental witch's altar is usually varied depending on their favored elements. Metals may be featured on these altars in many ways: gold pyramids; iron wands and bells; copper spheres and triangles; and silver chains for pendulums and talismans are common, as are gold, silver, and copper colors in artwork, candles, and other items.

Altars may also include elemental or alchemical symbols that are particularly useful or meaningful to the witch, with one of the most common being the four triangles representing the four main elements, or the pentagram, which can represent the four elements and the fifth: spirit. Their corresponding colors, too, are often featured as intermingling or otherwise together, a symbol for the constant ebb and flow between each element. These colors include red for fire, yellow for air, green for earth, and blue for water.

Some elemental witches like to separate the elements and have sections of their altar that honor each. This may be on the actual altar, but it may also be on the shelves above the altar as well. If they honor deities that represent those elements, their imagery is on the altar as well.

GETTING STARTED (BEGINNER)

Elemental witches may begin this path by connecting to the elements and their relationships to one another to obtain a sense of the symbolism. Like nature witches, being in nature is a start. Elemental witches may take this a bit further by collecting snow or nails to place on their altars, or gathering scraps of copper and other metals from projects to place in little sachets to promote the metal's intention. They may have devoted spaces to each element in the households to honor them, much like we do for deities, and may incorporate the elements' symbols in sigils. If they are inclined to incorporate deities into their practice, they may begin researching deities related to the elements and add statues or other symbols related to those deities on their altars. When it comes to spells, they will look how the elements work together to symbolize the intention to be manifested.

Elements and Their Traits

We already know that the elements have particular traits, but each element reacts with the others to increase or decrease its traits. Fire can burn wood (earth) to symbolize adding passion to our lives when we become stuck in our old ways or overly practical. Similarly, blowing dirt or seeds into the wind symbolizes the lightheartedness of air inspiring the earth to loosen its tethers to rationality and objectivity. We can add water to fire to temper or intensify those passions. And we could float a feather (a symbol for air) in a little creek (water) to encourage feelings of renewal or rebirth. How you choose to have the elements interact is up to you. There is no right way, as long as you're clear about what you want your spell to manifest. After all, adding earth to fire can both symbolize the easing of aggressive feelings or drowning our passions in rational thinking with two very different outcomes.

❧ Snow Spell for Emotional Release

When working with any element, consider how it changes in certain scenarios. There's no better place to start than with ice. Ice is water, the element of emotion, and so the symbolism of ice is stagnant or unwavering emotions. In working with ice or snow and letting it melt, we can encourage the movement of emotions to let them go, or we can use the symbolism to encourage us to be more open-minded with others' emotions. In this spell, we're working with fire and snow to ask for the bravery of fire to help us work through emotions.

When to perform this spell:
Saturday, any time (between 9 p.m. and 11 p.m. is ideal)

Ingredients/tools:
8-ounce (240-ml) glass jar
Ice or snow
Taper or chime candle, light blue

1. Fill about half (ideal) of the glass jar with snow.

2. Light the candle and slowly place it near the snow, allowing the candle to drip into the snow to heat and melt it. Move the candle deosil (clockwise). As you do this, state, "The state of fire conjures strength to move the moods that sadness makes."

3. Try to melt all the snow. When finished, pour the snow onto the earth (even if it is covered in snow) and state, "The ebb and flow begins again; let go of stagnant pain within."

4. Gather any wax that has fallen from the jar and throw away. (Some witches like to keep the wax bits from spells in a separate jar and discard them in a larger fire or throw away.)

Metal Corrosion

One of the most common ways elemental witches work with metals is through iron rust. Iron is a symbol of protection, but when it rusts (or when it's used symbolically to "nail" or "maim" an item), it can also symbolize the corrosion or ending of something. Beginning elemental witches can include this into their practice by simply using iron nails.

✣ Iron Nail Spell for Bad Habits

In this spell iron nails are enchanted to represent a habit at hand. As the nails slowly rust, the habit will be removed from the person afflicted by it.

When to perform this spell:
Saturday, any time (between 9 p.m. and 11 p.m. is ideal)

Ingredients/tools:
3 iron nails
Pine essential oil (see page 64)
Carrier oil of choice (see page 64)
Black twine

1. Anoint each nail with the pine and carrier oil mixture, using your thumb and pointer finger. Start from the middle and work your way down and around the nail. Then, start from the middle and work your way up.

2. Tie all the nails together, wrapping the twine three times around.

3. Secure the twine with a knot and then knot it twice more, for a total of three knots. As you do this, envision the habit you wish to end and state, "The knot for beginnings long ago. The middle's the bridge and across it I go. For the ending is the third, and with it this habit. As it rusts in the earth, the earth can now have it."

4. Bury your nails and twine in the southern direction of your property, or in a container pot.

Divinations

The elements are wise and truly ancient, as are the elementals that govern them. We can call upon the elements just as we would spirits, deities, or ancestors, and ask them for messages to help guide us in the future.

❦ Snow Divination

Snow offers us a blank canvas to spot messages on. In a classic divinatory process, we can "cast" something onto the snow and interpret any symbols, letters, or numbers we'd like for insight. Remember that these symbols are culturally tethered and personal to you, so the symbols you spot may relate to your belief system, such as animals that represent deities important to you or to a person or animal you know. Always offer thanks after any divinatory method in which spirits or energies are called upon.

When to perform this spell:
Monday, any time (3 p.m., 9 p.m., or 10 p.m. are ideal)

Ingredients/tools:
Snow
9 x 9-inch (23 x 23 cm) pan, or a 3 x 3-foot (1 x 1 m)
　　area of snow-covered ground
Dish filled with water

1.　As you place the snow into the pan (or as you find a plot of snow-covered ground), call the elements and ask for their presence stating, "As ancient as mountains that clamor to spirit. As primal as waters that move the earth near it. As lively as flames that flicker to being. As fickle as feathers when the air is caught fleeing. I call upon spirits embedded within, in hopes for some insight these elements send."

2.　Dip your hand into the dish of water and asperge (sprinkle or flick) the water outward five times in random and intuitive movements. This will cause divots in the snow.

3.　Look for any symbols to interpret.

INTERMEDIATE ELEMENTAL WITCHES

Intermediate elemental witchery takes the above concepts but adds more processes and takes into consideration the additional relationships, or changes, the elements go through to incorporate them into the magic. This requires more knowledge about the elements and how they interact with each other to bring about change on a chemical, or microscopic, level. This level of elemental magic also takes into consideration eventual changes caused by elemental interactions, such as how water eats away at earth over time, as well as using the nuances of elemental interactions as metaphors. If you would like to let your intuition guide you rather than using rational, earth-inspired practicality, you may want to combine the earth and water elements. However, water can slowly and softly alter stone in irrevocable ways, such as when hagstones are created in tumbling creeks. Or water can rush through a landscape and cause intense mudslides. These are the nuances of the elements, and they are just as important as the general elemental correspondences.

Chemical Reactions

Iron may rust, which is a chemical reaction, but other common witchy metals also undergo this process. Copper, which corresponds to healing, undergoes one of the most noticeable changes through chemical reactions with air over time. In fact, that's what makes the beautiful green patina on copper items. We can speed up this process by adding vinegar and salt and awaiting more immediate changes. The blue color that emerges is a bit of color correspondence, which contains a healing energy within itself.

⚘ Copper Healing Spell

Use this spell when you want to bring about healing, new beginnings, and emotional cleansing.

When to perform this spell:
Thursday, any time (10 p.m. is ideal for healing)

Ingredients/tools:
Bits of copper shavings (about the size of the tip of a pen)
Clear-glass jar
½ cup (100 g) salt
½ cup (125 ml) vinegar
Copper spoon
Light-blue, gray, or white piece of cloth
Blue-glass jar with lid

1. Add the copper shavings to the clear-glass jar, and then add salt. Lastly, add the vinegar and stir deosil (clockwise) nine times using a copper spoon.

2. Allow the shavings to sit for about an hour, and then remove and place on the cloth. Allow them to sit until chemical changes begin to appear.

3. Once the changes are seen, collect the shavings and add them to the blue-glass jar, secure the lid, and store. Whenever needed, sprinkle the copper shavings across the threshold of the home or keep the jar near the bedroom door. Before placing or sprinkling state, "The alchemist knows that change will win; I ask for some healing to conjure within."

The Domino Effect

The elements work together constantly, ebbing and flowing within and around each other and colliding to create newness and bring change. Sometimes a reaction can be a bit linear, and one element can cause a reaction in another, which causes change in yet another. Witches can harness this domino effect to bring about more complex change. Rather than controlling only one element and its traits, elemental witches can control all of the elements and manipulate the order in which they impact each other to encourage change.

❧ Elements Spell for Inevitable Change

Inevitable change, or large changes, are often the result of multiple elements coming together. In this spell, all the elements are incorporated to help handle changes, whether you initiated them or not. The candle is the initial spark of action and change.

When to perform this spell:

Wednesday, any time (2 p.m. or 6 p.m. are ideal)

Ingredients/tools:
Chime candle, brown
Feather
Shallow dish of water, filled to the brim
Dish of soil, filled to the brim
Candleholder
Palmful of thyme seeds

1. Place the items in the following order: chime candle, feather, dish of water, dish of soil. The dishes should be touching. Light the candle and secure it in the candleholder.

2. Using soft, slow movements, flick the flame and smoke with the feather upward and toward the direction of the dish with water. Say, "The winds come forth and with them change, but the elements guard to wall off pain. The child of air brings the will to change, and I pick myself up to begin again. Fire breathes to ignite the passion. To conjure my strength and forge the bastion. But water's high times will soften the brawn, and in comes compassion like a low, gentle song. And when I root down into Earth Mother's soil, I see all things clearly amid all this toil."

3. Flick the feather closer to the water. As the feather touches the water, it begins to flick water onto the soil. Feel free to "scoop" up water with the feather to fling onto the soil. Continue until the soil is decently damp on the top.

4. Plant the thyme seeds in the middle of the dish of soil. Place the dish in bright indirect light and keep the soil damp to initiate growth. As the plant grows, so too will the intention.

Tools for the Elemental Witch

In addition to the tools on pages 64–65, elemental witches may also use these.

TOOL	PROPERTIES
Metal pyramids and spheres	Metal pyramids and spheres can be hollow and non-hollow. They are heavy tools placed on crystal grids, in circles, or on altars that are used to hold (spheres) and channel (pyramids) energy when performing a spell. They are made from metal or metal-plated material.
Dowsing rods	Dowsing rods are metal rods, used in pairs, to perform spirit communication. When held by the witch, they will either cross or stay parallel to each other, indicating a "yes/no" answer from the divine.
Glass	Glass is a combination of sand and fire, a combination of the fire and earth elements. It's perfect in spells for grounding unchecked passion and transformations.
Wrought iron wands	Made by repeated hammering of iron when it's heated by fire. These hold and direct the energy of the fire element while offering protection.
Pentagram	Pentagrams symbolize the connectedness of the elements and the spiritual realm. Altar cloths, metal plaques, and even drawn pentagrams bring the energy to your altar.
Ice and Snow	Ice and snow represent stagnant or halted emotional flow. We can collect in glass jars for optimum combination of elements (fire, water, earth).
Mud	Mud combines the earth and water elements to help root our emotions in rationality, or to encourage us to let our intuition, rather than pragmatism, guide us. We often collect mud in dishes and draw sigils or symbols in them.
Ash	Ashes combine the earth, fire, and air elements and can be used to draw sigils when ground with mortar and pestle.

CHAPTER 5

HEARTH & HOME WITCHES

Hearth and home witches are drawn to creating sacred spaces and crafting magic with tools and ingredients often found in and around the home. These types of witches often practice traditional and folk magic, as well as kitchen witchery and cottage witchery, which we'll dive into in a bit. But no matter what they incorporate, the home—the safety, prosperity, happiness, and health—is the focus of this magic.

THE HEARTH AND HOME

A hearth is generally considered the part of the home that holds the fire, and where many home traditions and daily activities were completed. Traditionally, the hearth was in the center of the home but, today, we might consider this the fireplace (key word: might). On most fireplaces, you'll find stonework surrounding it, called the hearth. It's this place that we refer to in our history of hearth witchcraft, but it's not the only space hearth witches use in the home to perform their magic. They may use any part of the house, or any land or gardens around it.

Hearth witches are often homebodies, and they appreciate the history of their homes and the land, so you'll often find them incorporating elements from their immediate environment, such as local flora and fauna, into their work. Hearth witches can be rather solitary, but they may also enjoy the benefits of a tight-knit community and of a strong family and nearby kin. In this way, the hearth witch can be seen as a folk witch in that their magic includes a heavy focus on the community and its longevity.

Hearth witches may also utilize local folklore from their region in their magic. If located in a seaport town, the hearth witch may employ magic to protect the community's fishers from rough winds and storms. The hearth witch may visit local spiritually charged areas, such as holy wells or haunted buildings, to ask for blessings of regional entities. Stones may be charged at the crossroads on the outskirts of town. For the hearth witch, community and locality are a huge part of the practice. Hearth witches also follow the flow of the seasons, much like nature witches do. They harvest and plant according to the propensities of the area, and they follow the phases of the moon and the timeline of the sun to help guide their chores. They may favor sowing seeds of plants native to the region, and they know when high and low tides are expected.

As important as the home itself is to the hearth witch, the garden is equally important. This is the space where culinary and magical tools are grown. Hearth witches look to this garden to provide sustenance in both matters. The enchantment may always venture back into the home, but it's born in the garden as much as the home.

For hearth witches, areas of the home double in their purpose: kitchens are places to simmer intention and dinners for the family. Thresholds, such as front doors and kitchen windows, are places where protective magic, like witch bottles and sigils, might be placed. Brooms sweep the floors, ushering out bad energy and cleansing the space spiritually. Each of these spaces is important in the overall functionality of the home, in both a physical and spiritual sense, and so the hearth witch doesn't just focus on the hearth, which the name suggests. Each room holds the essence of the person or people who frequent it, and so each room is a space in which magic can be done to foster the health and happiness of the family.

As such, the magic that arises from hearth witchery often focuses on the qualities that make a happy home: safety, prosperity, happiness, health, peace, kindness, cleansing, fertility, sensuality, love, and protection. Of course, the hearth witch may venture out of these intentions. No witch is limited in the intentions that can be used. But, for hearth witches, these take precedence.

A Brief History of Magic in the Home

Because of the nature of witchcraft, we can't be truly certain of when magic in the home began, but we can be certain the concept of the "cunning woman" can be traced by grave artifacts well into the sixth century. Cunning women, and men, too, were those who provided the community with healing and with magical support, such as finding lost livestock and identifying thieves. Countermagic? The cunning folk in your community could help you. Need a strong poultice? Seek out the village cunning woman. These cunning folk permeated the Old World well into the 1800s and, surely, beyond. So, there has always been magic in the home. It just depends on the context. We have plenty of evidence, and not just in graves, that points to magical workings in the home. In the Old World and in the New World, artifacts provide evidence of some sort of ritualistic goings-on in the home, like protection and prosperity of all members of the home. Research points us to bottles, shoes, worn clothing, and poppets (little dolls in this case) buried in the chimney, attic, and around the stonework in mantels. These items were always well worn, to the point of rags, and sometimes they were found where there would be no purpose for them, like in wells or in areas *not* used by builders. Little scratches of symbols in woodwork on barns and homes. These proliferated in Europe's homes and, later, colonial American homes, indicating immigrants brought these practices with them to their new homes. Though, the artifacts don't share just how much magic went on behind closed doors, as much of the evidence is long since gone.

We see possible evidence of these findings in tales of witch trials. In Salem, Massachusetts, alone, Bridget Bishop would be accused of hiding poppets in her walls, and Mary Sibley would be the instigator behind the countermagic of the witch cake, made and fed to the dog to identify the witch responsible for the bewitched girls' ailment that started it all.

The hearth and home were feminine domains, guarded by the females who performed domestic chores. Females young and old did everything in this sphere, from tending the cooking over the hearth and cleaning the laundry to preserving the harvest and aiding the dying, often kin of others in their homes. And so we cannot ignore that when *any* goings-on in these areas went awry, they were sometimes considered magic, and the woman considered a witch—such as herbal healing that didn't work out right; births met with sad endings; or homes alight with random fires in the middle of the night. And it's in these moments, when all goes left, that we can imagine the human condition uttering some sort of plea to the universe for relief. So, the spectrum of magic we know is, perhaps, limited, but make no mistake: There was magic in the home, and those who employed it.

UNIQUE ASPECTS OF HEARTH WITCHES

Hearth witches stand out among other witches because they carry the torch of these familial home-based practices. Whereas other witches may relocate to the ocean or the middle of the forest to perform nature magic, or some witches may don a robe with their coven and practice rites of initiation in a communal area, the house witch performs magic in the comfort of the home. Although all kinds of witches can carry on traditions passed down, hearth witches may be considered the forerunners because their magic likely already pulls from the folklore of the region, the tips and recipes passed down from family, and more.

Tools for the Hearth Witch

TOOL	DESCRIPTION	PROPERTIES
Ash	Ashes come from the fireplace, and we powder them using a mortar and pestle.	Ashes are protective and can be used in lieu of salt. They are also a combination of fire and earth elements, symbolizing earth's ability to calm stormy thoughts and unbridled passions.
Blankets	Blankets, often made of wool, are sources of comfort readily available in the home.	Blankets can be enchanted to encourage certain intentions for a specific family member, like happiness for children.
Firewood	The most common firewood is oak, a sacred tree, but maple can also be used.	Burning these woods is a spell in itself, sending the intentions out to the ether to be manifested. Oak symbolizes strength and courage; maple symbolizes prosperity.
Flowers and herbs	Flowers and herbs are the hearth witch's go-to for correspondences to add to spells. We may dress candles with these, burn them, sprinkle them, or cook with them.	All flowers have different correspondences; a list of intentions is ideal for the hearth witch to have on hand (see pages 116–117).
Gardening tools	Gardening tools may include hoes, spades, trowels, and shears. These could be hand-size, making them perfect for working more intimately with plants.	Much like the besom and cauldron, a witch's gardening tools can double as wands to direct energy, or use "burying" tools in banishing spells.

Tools for the Hearth Witch *(continued)*

TOOL	DESCRIPTION	PROPERTIES
Mantels and shelves	The mantel is the shelf above the fire used to house mementos. We can always use wooden shelves, whether there is a fireplace underneath or not.	Mantels and shelves offer an alternative altar; there, we can craft a space that promotes hearth witch intentions, like abundance. We can use each shelf for a separate intention, or as places of remembrance for ancestors.
Mason jars	Mason jars come in different sizes and their clear nature allows us to readily identify the plant material or other items kept inside them.	Glass itself is a witch's tool; its coloring (amber, clear, blue) can add correspondence; glass speaks to the earth element of stability and grounding, as it's made partly of sand and limestone.
Pottery	Pottery, ideally handmade, is often found in the hearth witch's kitchen and garden.	Pottery is part of the earth element, and so it brings stability into the home and, when used, encourages that intention in our lives.
Spoons	A good wooden spoon can operate as a kitchen witch's wand, directing the witch's energy into the food. Any size will do, but usually one spoon is designated as the "witch spoon."	Wooden spoons allow you to add a tree's intention to your recipes, such as birch for purity or maple for abundance. We can also have symbols, like protective sigils or moon phases, inscribed into the wood.
Wooden well bucket	Buckets are great for the practical purposes of gathering large harvests of herbs, flowers, and mast (see page 117).	The well bucket can double as a scrying bowl by placing water in it and performing a scrying spell.
Yarns, string, and other textiles	These bits of textiles are often from torn blankets and clothes, family crafts, and decor.	These textiles offer sympathetic magic for any items used in magic (think poppets) that represent people in the home.

Focused Pathway 6
Kitchen Witch

A kitchen witch is a hearth witch who finds magic in cooking up intentions. The recipes often include little chants or acts of magic, like stirring the spoon deosil (clockwise) or widdershins (counterclockwise) to infuse recipes with intention. And when we nibble that food, we are quite literally placing that intention into ourselves.

Kitchen witches aren't limited to cooking; indeed, some kitchen witches don't enjoy cooking elaborate witchy meals. Some prefer the simplicity and efficiency that kitchen witchery brings. After all, we all have to eat anyway, and so the busy, efficient witch may see a simple lunch as a way to eat and manifest magic at the same time. These kinds of kitchen witches find enjoyment from crafting teas and coffees, turning their toast into pallets of abundance on which any corresponding vegetable, fruit, and sugared substance can add intention. Whether your kitchen witchery is elaborate or not, we can begin the path with simple recipes.

GETTING STARTED (BEGINNER)

Beginner kitchen witches come in different types—either foodies and recipe aficionados who want to pair their culinary prowess with their magic, or those who want to explore a different way to infuse their life with magic. Both types will likely begin by understanding food correspondences (see pages 108–109), typically ingredients that can be incorporated into a multitude of recipes, such as flour, sugar, oats, and more. They may also begin by focusing on basics, like quick drinks, syrups, and salads, which don't take much time to practice and can build confidence in pairing foods and their intentions successfully. Indeed, kitchen witches have to think about the flavor of their foods as well as how the intentions come together. After all, tomatoes and figs may both promote fertility, but they may not taste good together. The kitchen witch develops the skill of pairing both for taste and intention.

The beginner kitchen witch can also pay attention to rather benign additions to their magic, like stirring their spoons in a certain direction, blowing on their food, or adding little symbols in their recipes. We may stir foods intended to add something to our lives, like love or money, clockwise, also called "deosil". Or, we

may stir them counterclockwise, or "widdershins," to remove something from our lives, like banishing habits, letting go of negative feelings or cleansing. Witches may add to their intentions by blowing on their food while they envision the intention at hand, like feeling safe or loved. And they may also add subtle intentions by "drawing" a moon phase with the ingredients before stirring them in. These little additions are quick, but each adds a little "oomph" to the kitchen witchery.

Enchanted Teas, Soups, and Meldings

Simple drinks, such as tea, are a great place to begin, as they allow us to customize the recipe quickly, and there is no great loss if the flavors don't pan out. But what makes tea special is that it's an ancient drink that allows us to connect to tradition, which may appeal to the hearth witch in particular. Tea, or *Camellia sinensis*, is considered a sacred plant connected with Buddha and monks. It was said to be used in meditative practice to keep the practitioner awake. That spiritual component makes tea perfect for the kitchen witch, especially the busy one who would like to focus on spirituality but doesn't have much time to do so. To the tea, we can add any correspondence we like. Lavender, hops, and lemon balm are perfect additions for calming teas, and honeysuckle teas are perfect for protection. And there is certainly no shortage of tonics and elixirs we can add to teas to amp up their power. Teas aren't the only option here; soups offer the same versatility and ease. We can combine nearly anything we'd like into the pot and allow it to meld together, thereby melding your intentions to create something truly specific to your magical needs.

🌿 Abundance Tea

Infuse your day with motivation, abundance, and prosperity by crafting a spicy citrus blend of tea. While any chai tea can offer abundance, adding citrus offers a jolt of motivation to achieve that abundance.

When to perform this spell:
Any day, preferably in the morning

Ingredients/tools:
1 cup (240 ml) hot water

Mug

Spoon

1 tablespoon loose black tea, such as Ceylon

2 whole cloves

1 teaspoon grated orange peel

¼ teaspoon ground cinnamon

Tea ball or strainer

1. Pour the water into a mug, and stir it deosil (clockwise) 3 times.

2. Place the tea, cloves, orange peel, and cinnamon into a loose tea holder, such as a tea ball. Bob the ball in the water and inhale slowly, letting the smell of the citrus and spice take over your senses. Place your face close to the steam, letting it envelop the face.

3. Let the tea steep for 5 to 10 minutes.

4. Stir the tea 3 times again, deosil (clockwise), by rotating the tea ball in the water. Remove the tea ball.

5. Hold the mug in both hands and whisper into the water, "Steam meets tongue and so it is; abundance for me, for home, for kin."

6. Enjoy, sipping the tea slowly.

INTERMEDIATE KITCHEN WITCHCRAFT

Intermediate witches may want to move beyond the creation of teas and other liquids and venture into crafting tonics and herbal medicines. Crafting herbal medicines should be performed only after serious study about the qualities of various herbs and how they interact with the body, as well as an understanding of how they may interact with medications*. As you can imagine, that's a lofty undertaking and a serious one. There are many courses offered by qualified herbalists to help guide you down this intermediate path. However, you may move into intermediate kitchen witchery without taking on this additional profession of herbal healer. You can incorporate ready-made tinctures and tonics crafted by qualified herbalist into your crafted goodies, and there's nothing wrong with that. You can also begin making herbal concoctions.

*__Safety Note:__ *Consult your medical practitioner before using any herbs.*

Herbal Vinegars and Oils

Crafting herbal vinegars and oils moves up one step further from teas in that they're steeped for longer periods of time, allowing them to strengthen and build in intention. We watch over them and stir them daily, adding our vibrations to the concoction each time we do this. In this process, we spend more time catering to our magic, becoming more knowledgeable of the flavors and combinations of herbs and flowers and so on. This "intimacy" between witch and correspondences is an intermediate approach, as beginners may focus less on the partnership between witch and the craft and more on the result. Herbal vinegars vary in their inclusions, from sweet and tangy salad vinegars to hearty herbal oils for potato dishes. And you can even soak herbs in alcohol for inclusion in teas, sparkling waters, and alcoholic beverages.

❧ Cleansing Herbal Oil

Use this oil on salads, potatoes, roasted vegetables, and more to add the intention of cleansing and purity to your magic. If you'd like it to have a bit more bite, replace the oil with vinegar. In this way, you ensure that whatever intentions you want to manifest are done honestly and in good faith.

When to perform this spell:
Any day, but preferably Saturday, any time (1 p.m. or 8 p.m. are ideal)

Ingredients/tools:
¼ cup (12 g) dried lemon thyme leaves
1 tablespoon dried basil leaves
Pinch of dried marjoram
One 16-ounce (475 ml) Mason jar with a lid and seal
1 cup (240 ml) olive oil or (224 g) coconut oil
Wooden spoon

1. Add each herb individually to the jar, being mindful of what each will bring to your home: lemon thyme for cleansing; basil for healing; and marjoram for happiness.

2. As you add each, state its intentions aloud and envision what the home will feel like with these intentions manifested. For instance, you may envision your children laughing as you add the marjoram.

3. Pour in the oil to coat the herbs and stir the oil deosil (clockwise) with the wooden spoon.

4. Close the seal and lid and give the oil a good shake. As you do, state, "Coat the harvest with garden magic; as we eat, as we have it."

5. Place the jar in a cool, dark, dry place and shake it every day for 3 to 4 weeks. Then strain the oil through a fine-mesh sieve. Store in a cool, dark, dry place as well.

Nuances of the Kitchen Witch

The intermediate witch may also work with heating and cooling as symbols in their magic, such as freezing or blanching vegetables to halt gossip or end a spell, or heating up love correspondences to add sensuality and speed to the spell. These are all additional bits of symbolism that the beginner witch, perhaps, doesn't think about, but that can be include in rituals to strengthen them. It is, technically, kitchen witchery to bind a cow's tongue and stick it in the freezer to freeze the lips of a gossiper, isn't it? Although you may not be snagging cow parts any time soon, any of these little additions improves your kitchen witch repertoire.

❦ Beet Love Spell

Beets correspond to love and we can utilize heat in kitchen witchery to strengthen the attachment and passion that comes with love. Its status as a root vegetable furthers its correspondence to love, as it's only through sturdy roots that attachments stay strong.

When to perform this spell:
Friday, any time (3 p.m. or 10 p.m. are ideal)

Ingredients/tools:
Rimmed baking sheet
Aluminum foil
3 beets, peeled
1 tablespoon melted coconut oil
¼ cup (80 g) chopped sweet onion
¼ teaspoon ground white pepper
¼ teaspoon ground coriander

1. Preheat the oven to 400°F (200°C). Line a baking sheet with aluminum foil.

2. Tear off 3 sheets of foil, each 8 inches (20 cm) in width, and place 1 beet onto each sheet. Curl up the edges of the foil so the beet is in a "nest."

3. In the small bowl, toss together the oil, onion, pepper, and coriander. Drizzle some of the mixture over each beet, envisioning roots deepening into the soil, and state, "As it is in Mother Earth, so it be within this hearth." Enclose each beet in its foil sheet and place the wrapped beets on the prepared baking sheet.

4. Bake for about 1 hour, checking them periodically, or until soft.

Food Correspondences

All foods have individual intentions, and many authors have crafted books devoted to sharing each correspondence. To begin our kitchen witchery journey, start by understanding what "groups" of foods offer in a broad sense. Then, if you choose to get more specific, seek out more detailed lists. Following is a list of broad correspondences of common kitchen witchery inclusions.

Food Correspondences

TOOL	DESCRIPTION	PROPERTIES
Citrus fruits	Citrus fruits include clementines, grapefruit, kumquats, lemons, limes, and tangerines.	These fruits correspond to purification, cleansing, and love
Flour	Flour, much like bread, is considered sacred, and we use flours to thicken soups and bake goods.	Use flour to craft protective circles in the kitchen, as well as heighten spirituality by nibbling flour-based goodies.
Greens	Here, "greens" refers to green vegetables, ranging from cabbage, lettuce, and broccoli to spinach, kale, and celery.	Use these green vegetables in protection, peace, and prosperity spells.
"Intense" spices	We can group spices based on flavor, and these include hot or intense spices such as black pepper, chile powder, cinnamon, clove, coriander, ginger, and mace.	These spices correspond to money, success, and protection.
Nightshades	Nightshades include tomatoes, potatoes, peppers, and eggplant. These vegetables are in the same family as the witch's coveted, and toxic, plant belladonna*. *Safety Note: We do not recommend nor advocate using any toxic plants in this book.	Nightshades connect us to darker, or shadow magic, where we reflect on the self and, perhaps, ask gods and goddesses to support a painful healing journey.

Food Correspondences *(continued)*

TOOL	DESCRIPTION	PROPERTIES
Nuts	Nuts include almonds, cashews, coconuts, hazelnuts, peanuts, pecans, walnuts, and more.	Nuts, generally, correspond to money.
Oats, hops, and grains	Oats, hops, and grains can be incorporated into our diets via beer (another sacred food), breads, cereals, oatmeal, and more.	Although they have their individual correspondences, these foods all, in general, offer prosperity, abundance, and fertility.
Root vegetables	Root vegetables range from beets and carrots to parsnips, onions, and potatoes.	Root vegetables connect us to the abundance of earth and to ancestors, as they are metaphorical "roots" into the hardy soil on which we all live.
Salt	Salt, along with pepper, is a common inclusion in savory dishes, and the kitchen witch may use it as an inclusion rather than a protective device in nonkitchen magic.	Salt always offers protection, but it can correspond to prosperity and the earth element, which means it works for spells in which rationality and objective reasoning are needed.
Stone fruits	These fruits include apricots, peaches, plums, and nectarines.	Stone fruits relate to love and fertility. In addition to eating the fruit, save and dry the stone to use in your magic.
Sugar, syrups, and honey	Sugar, syrups, and honey are common additions to sweet pastries and teas.	These inclusions are sacred and are often considered offerings to deities, entities, and spirits. They also "sweeten" (strengthen) spells.
Tea and coffee	Tea and coffee are sacred drinks, revered for their spiritual heightening.	Sip before any divination ritual to add power and spiritual connection.

Focused Pathway 7
Cottage Witch

The cottage witch is a hearth witch who, perhaps, focuses more on the gardening and cultivating aspects of hearth witchery. Whereas the kitchen witch preserves the fruits, the cottage witch plants the herbs and harvests the fruits, harvests and hangs the herbs to dry, and performs magic related to the sowing of the seed, the fertility of the ground, and the thriving of the flowers used in nonfood magic. Think of both the kitchen witch and the cottage witch as integral parts of hearth witchery, and although they can perform the same witchy duties, each tends to focus on different parts of hearth witchcraft. Much like the kitchen witch, the cottage witch focuses primarily on everyday magic—health, security, happiness, peace, protection, and love. They may share their flowers and herbs with others in the community and craft ointments and other herbal healing goodies that help take care of family and kin. In that, we see the same community focus as the kitchen witch.

GETTING STARTED (BEGINNER)

Cottage witches are also likely to cultivate a garden, either in containers, raised beds, or next to the hearth in a fenced-off garden. They may also focus on the landscape surrounding the hearth to see where they can incorporate their magic. And they're likely to place these plants strategically, using color and lore in their choices. This doesn't have to be the place to start, but the cottage witch's green thumb and love of flora and fauna mean they are pulled toward this space. Make no mistake: Cottage witches enjoy the comfort of the hearth fire, the magic of a comforting quilt, and a good cup of tea. They are not always inclined to be gardeners or florists. But the traditional medieval definition of the cottage indicates that a garden or plot of land was always present to feed the family who lived there and served a "lord" with the work. And so, cottage witches look to this plot of land as their focus.

Home and Family Cleansing and Protection

Protection and cleansing are essential to the cottage witch, and so a good deal of beginner cottage witchery is establishing strong protective borders and ensuring the space is cleansed spiritually and physically. This type of witch may place red begonias and cranberry bushes near the front of the home for protection and add flower boxes full of lemon balm and lavender outside bedroom windows for cleansing and calm. A good, sturdy besom is suggested for cleansing the space and bringing in good energy. This amounts to nothing more than enchanting the broom for such purposes.

❧ Cranberry Garland for Protection & Vitality

Garlands offer protection and power, much like braids or cords do. When crafting a garland, as you place each item, you build and intensify the intention. When hung outside, on the mantel, on curtain rods, or near the front door of the home, a garland adds the intention to the space. Here, we use cranberries, known for their cottage witch intentions of prosperity, protection, and healing.

When to perform this spell:
Saturday, at noon

Ingredients/tools:
Scissors
Twine
Needle
About 30 cranberries, ideally fresh or mid-dried
Other personal additions, such as apple or pear slices or candied ginger
    cubes, which all have the same correspondences as cranberries
Red thread (optional)

1. Snip off a length of twine 3 feet (90 cm) long. Tie one end into a knot and thread the other end into a needle.

2. Begin piercing the berries and other fruit or additions with the needle, one by one, in a pattern you like, pushing them to the knotted end of the twine.

3. If you'd like, tie a bit of red thread to the twine and, once done threading the twine through the items, thread the red string through. This adds protection.

4. Once finished, tie off the end and hold the garland in your hand while you whisper, "All's well in hearth and home, when hedgerow trinkets guard my own."

5. Hang as desired.

Intermediate Cottage Witchcraft

Intermediate cottage witches may focus more on the changes of the seasons and, thus, the changing of the land in which they cultivate their garden. They understand, much like green witches do, that the ground is just as important as the flowers and it, too, should be honored. They are likely to lay the ground to rest, giving the earth a nice blessing before it goes dormant for winter, or they mindfully tend the compost to help the earth with nutrients needed to keep the garden healthy. It's these more mindful, time-consuming acts that turn the cottage witch from beginner to intermediate because there is less focus on what the witch gets out of the spell and more focus on the spiritual partnership between the witch and the land. Intermediate cottage witches may also focus on hearth witch activities a bit more involved than crafting a quick garland. Just like the kitchen witch begins to focus on the nuances of stirring, heating, and cooling, the cottage witch may focus on more mindful activities, such as stitching and sewing.

Stitches and Sigils

Stitching intentions requires elongated visualization, and it's hard to sustain that kind of attention without losing track of your thoughts, especially in repetitive activities like stitching. That's what makes stitching more intermediate. It may seem simple enough, but as we stitch, we build intention, and if our mind ventures off into other things, like anxiety over work, we're accidentally stitching in those feelings, which muddies up the spellwork.

Stitching connects one piece of fabric or intention to another, so we can stitch pieces of fabric together to bring prospective lovers to meet. We can stitch someone's fabrics to offer emotional mending as well as physical healing, and we can stitch sigils, symbols that hold power to the witch and symbolize an intention, into textiles to attach a bit of intention to the wearer. And we're not limited to clothes; blankets, scarves, and so on are used to "coat" the person with your spell. We can also craft dollies, handkerchiefs, and other smaller items for people to carry.

☙ Stitching Stability

In this spell, stitches are added as a symbol of stability and foundation to our lives. Use any symbol you like, such as a tree limb, an oak leaf, or even just words that remind you of stability, like "grounding," "strength," and so on. Choose something meaningful to you or the person you're performing this spell for.

When to perform this spell:
Thursday, any time (5 p.m. or midnight are ideal)

Ingredients/tools:
Scissors
Thread in one of the following colors: black, brown, gray-green, or
 rusty orange
Needle
Textile to be stitched, such as a square of muslin fabric, a blanket, or a scarf

1. Thread the needle.

2. Situate yourself in a comfortable spot and close your eyes, swaying the body and holding the needle in one hand and the textile in the other.

3. If this spell is for you, envision yourself lying on the ground, roots stemming out of your feet and into earth. If it's for another, envision this person lying on the ground and in peace, their feet growing roots.

4. This imagery will continue, with roots that grow and strengthen, venturing further into the ground. Other parts of the body begin to grow roots as tethers into the ground. Maintain this visualization as you begin stitching the symbol or word you've chosen.

5. The trick is to maintain this visualization without breaking it. If necessary, envision what you smell, hear, see, and feel as well. This helps keep you in the vision by maintaining focus.

6. Continue until the stitching is done, and then knot the thread 3 times.

7. State, "A breath to change the path (they're/I'm) on. What's in my heart has now begun." Breathe a little breath onto the stitching.

8. Knot the thread one more time to seal the spell.

PLANT CORRESPONDENCES

We may think of the cottage witch as a master of wildflowers, but traditional cottage gardens featured cooking and medicinal herbs in the same garden as the flowers, and sometimes the right plant was found in the forest either on the ground or right beside us. And so cottage witches look to all kinds of plants* for magic, not just the flowers.

Safety Note: *Exercise caution with all plants and herbs, as allergic reactions are always a possibility and many can be toxic at high doses. Research each herb carefully, wear gloves when handling, and always wash hands after use.*

Plant Correspondences

PLANT	DESCRIPTION	PROPERTIES
Flowers	Dry flowers and sprinkle them on the floor at night to encourage intentions, burn them as loose incense, place them on the altar as an offering to deities, and infuse them into oils to anoint candles.	Plant native flowers in the garden to encourage the individual intentions while still honoring the region and its critters.
Lavender	Lavender's versatility, offered with its flower stems or as simple leaves, means we can use it as a floral bouquet for the mantel (a sneaky bit of magic), or to smoke cleanse the space.	Use lavender for calm, sleep, dreams, and luck. Sprinkle the flowers along thresholds of the bedroom or the cottage to encourage the intentions.

Plant Correspondences *(continued)*

PLANT	DESCRIPTION	PROPERTIES
Lemon balm, marjoram, and basil	These "soft" herbs add a gentle flavoring to foods and drinks.	All three herbs focus on healing, happiness, and calm.
Mast	Mast includes all the fruits and organic material that falls off plants, namely trees and bushes, including acorns, seeds, leaves, and fruit.	Gather and dry the mast and use it as an offering, or add it to abundance rituals by grinding the mast in a mortar and pestle and dressing candles with it.
Mint	Like thyme (see following), there are different kinds of mint, such as chocolate, orange, peppermint, pineapple, and spearmint.	Mint means cleansing, abundance, and purity.
Rosemary	Rosemary's sturdy stems and long leaves make it ideal for smoke cleanses and can be used much like sage.	Rosemary means ancestral connection, intellectual knowledge, remembrance, and wisdom.
Soil and dirt	Soil and dirt are different. Soil contains the nutrients that allow plants to thrive. Dirt does not contain those nutrients.	Use soil in abundance and fertility spells, and dirt in protective magic.
Thyme	Thyme comes in a variety of subtle flavors, such as lemon.	Thyme can be used for cleansing or children's magic (protection, safety, and happiness).
Tree leaves	Tree leaves, preferably dried, take on the correspondences of the tree they belong to. Gather these and place them in jars on the mantel to encourage intention.	Like flowers, trees have certain intentions, but they all share the intentions of abundance, obstacle removal, strength, and wisdom.

CHAPTER 6

INTUITIVE WITCHES

Witchcraft is a personal practice, a pathway to help us better understand the spiritual side of things, no matter what our craft focuses on. One result many witches hope for is a stronger spiritual self that helps guide us through life. This may include a stronger ability to speak to spirits and other entities, to tap into psychic abilities that don't involve the other side, and to bring the intuitive self closer to the surface, so we're better guided by our gut instincts in all we do. In essence, the intuitive witch *knows* things without gaining any outside information to help, and the way to build this skill is opening up to the spiritual side, within us and in the cosmos. The intuitive witch, then, works with tools, spells, and rituals that help foster this intuition, this ability to gather information or feelings and understand them without conscious thought, as definitions would suggest.

Intuitive witchcraft looks at this outcome less as a by-product of performing rituals and spells and more as a main focus of the craft. They can go about this in different ways, and that's what leads to different pathways. The cosmic witch uses celestial bodies to learn more about the self and to build intuitive awareness. Others interested in intuitive witchcraft may focus on speaking with spirits, and so this practice includes tools such as pendulums, spirit boards, tarot cards, and more that allow the spiritual side to speak. But is it always the spiritual side speaking? That's truly a question for the cosmos, as I am not sure anyone can really know. Sometimes, the gut responses we get that we attribute to our intuition may be spirits speaking to us on a subconscious level. Sometimes, it may be the intuition we've fostered, a very close sense of self, and the outside world that allows us to pick up the smallest details subconsciously. Or, maybe the feelings and answers we get are not the result of spiritual communication but, rather, energy being transferred between objects and people. We'll break this down a bit more when talking about psychic witches.

First, to understand intuition, we need to venture into where intuition comes from, whether you're speaking to spirits or listening to your gut. These thoughts, no matter who is sending them, are likely picked up and interpreted by the nonconscious self. They could be picked up by the subconscious, or the part of us that performs daily tasks and takes in information but doesn't consciously focus on it until we try. It's the subconscious that allows us to follow traffic rules even when we're deep in thought and don't remember the drive to work. It's the unconscious that houses the residual feelings, experiences, and latent desires hidden deep inside. And so intuition that is not from a spiritual source may be coming from these two areas.

No matter where the intuition originates, intuitive witches are, perhaps, more inclined to focus on shadow work. Discussed more in depth following, shadow work is the conscious effort to sift through the subconscious and unconscious realms of self to heal and to let go of traits, habits, and ways of being not exactly in line with who we want to be. Intuitive witches, in an attempt to get closer to the core spiritual, intuitive self, may engage in shadow work as a way to move through the blockages that keep them from meeting that self. Intuition is inside us all, just as we all have a conscious, subconscious, and unconscious self. We can hone our intuition just like any other skill. But how would we actively work with these parts of ourselves to bring about change? In essence, how does the witch "work" with these parts of the self?

WORKING WITH INTUITION

Because the intuitive witch works with the inner spaces of the self that hide beneath the surface, they are likely going to incorporate the water element and the moon into their rituals and spells. The water element controls these aspects of being and helps us make sense of them, and the moon controls the tides. In this symbolism, then, the moon helps us yield loving power and control over our emotions and better understand what the intuitive self is saying so we can make wise, gut-informed decisions.

Planets are also a part of the intuitive witch's practice. Like all other natural elements, the planets have correspondences, too, and these can relate to what the intuitive witch wants to focus on, such as removing obstacles, tempering emotions, and so on. The intuitive witch may use the correspondences and positions of the planets to help them choose the times at which they perform any magic. Using the moon is similar; therefore, the intuitive witch inscribes or otherwise incorporates the phases of the moon, much like the planets, when considering the timing of spells.

These witches may also use water as a way to "see" into the self, connect with spirits, or scry the future. They may use water charged in a certain moon phase to asperge (sprinkle with water) their tools, like ceremonial drums, wands, candles, and crystals. And they may use teas (waters) and herbs* for psychic awareness to enhance spellwork.

Safety Note: *Be sure to research carefully any herbs used and read the manufacturer's instructions when applying or ingesting any type of herb.*

It makes sense that intuitive witches engage in spells and rituals geared toward fostering their understanding of the self and inner motives. This means they are likely to engage in dream magic, where they can look at the needs and desires of the unconscious self and use that knowledge to help guide their magic. For instance, an intuitive witch may perform some dream magic in the hopes of having lucid dreams, or dreams wherein they control the dream's outcome because they understand they're in a dream state. They may pay attention to symbols that emerge in those dreams, the people involved, or the event at hand, and use that information to perform healing spells for themselves concerning that event.

They also work to find the connection between mind, body, and spirit. And so the go-to practices in this kind of witchery are meditation, trance, and visualization. These practices require the witch to venture inward and pick up on nuances in the body to strengthen their intuition and inner guidance. They may, for instance, focus on the tempo and strength of breath when envisioning something. They may venture into the otherworld, or the realm of spirits and deities, to gain ancestral insight and awareness into how they connect to the universe as a whole and how they can better know themselves. And they may place the body in trancelike states to foster tranquility and peace to calm the body, mind, and spiritual self.

Intuitive witches also use clairvoyance to garner information, and this involves less of a connection with spiritual entities and more of a honing into the mind and the subtle energies softly dancing about that space to gain insight and information. We'll discuss clairvoyance in a bit. Intuitive witches don't just venture inward, but it's those skills to do so that help them in the outside world. For instance, intuitive witches who take the time to explore the nuances of breath in the body and identify where their energy sits in the body also strengthen their ability to pick up on the little twinges of feeling when entering a new space, and the subtle movements of energy, like a small breeze over the arm when near a sacred space such as an altar or holy well. In their inner work, they build that sense of focus on intricate details that help them better identify when there are energies, even subtle ones, nearby. Couple this with spiritual journeys, and you have the makings for psychic magic.

A Brief History of Intuitive Magic

Intuitive magic involves a great deal of spiritual communication and divination, and these are concepts that stem back to early civilizations; we've always been trying to contact or appease the spiritual side. Again, we can look to the ancient Celts or shamanic practices of a variety of cultures tens of thousands of years ago to see those attempts at spiritual journeys and connection.

For an interesting look at when these practices may have become more widely accepted or popularized, we can look to the Victorian age, or the 1800s, when many forms of divination or spiritual communication permeated society thanks to the industrial revolution. This meant mass production of items such as the Ouija board, planchettes, automatic writing tools, tea leaf reading tools, crystal balls, tarot decks, and so on proliferated the homes of the middle classes on both sides of the sea. Although these items were used more for filling time and entertaining guests at parties, we do see the emergence of seance performers and those making money off their spiritual communications. Many of these practices were fraught with fraud, but we can argue that the Spiritualist movement that underpinned these interests exposed people to these methods of spiritual communication and made them a bit easier to perform. The Spiritualist movement reached its height in the mid-1800s, and its main tenet was their ability to communicate with the dead. Although communicating with the dead isn't all the intuitive witch does, it is certainly a part of it. Intuitive witches meditate, divine, and otherwise contact the cosmos for guidance. It makes sense that those on the other side, be they ghosts, ancestors or simply energy, contact them back.

However, although meditation is an archaic art that strengthens the mind-spirit-body connection, we can see the re-emergence of the practice as "popular" in the 1960s and 1970s, right in line with the New Age movement, which included a variety of spiritual beliefs and practices making it difficult to describe, even by scholars. But at its heart, New Age subscribers believed in spiritual transformation and healing brought about by the practitioner, the cosmos, and the celestial bodies therein, divine beings and the interconnectedness of humanity. The New Age movement focused on the spiritual self as an integral part of such transformation, and that the radical change needed to shift the world to a more connected, spirited state would eventually lead to the New Age. The connectedness of the self to the spiritual side was of great focus, but in the latter years of the movement, the focus became less on the interconnectedness of humanity and the universe, and more on the self in particular.

Those in New Age communities engaged in spiritual practices, like yoga and meditation, healing, communing with spirits, and working with crystals and other sources of cosmic energy. The movement would begin to wane in the 1980s, but its impact was already prevalent in Western society, and its broad spiritualism but lack of definitive, specific belief systems made it the backbone for intuitive witchcraft as well as eclectic and niche practices (see chapter 7).

New Age understandings, interestingly enough, furthered the spiritual ideas found in the 1800s, an understanding that there was hidden spiritual knowledge out there ready to be obtained if the human being, part of the cosmos, was open enough to receive it. Because of the New Age movement being an overriding spiritual concept rather than a set of specific tenets and belief practices, it is considered "eclectic" and many witches look to practices that can be considered "New Age" because they are broad enough to allow everyone to feel included.

UNIQUE ASPECTS OF INTUITIVE WITCHES

Intuitive witches are able to tap into the self more easily than other witches who focus on the world around them. This means they likely have an easier time venturing into meditation or trance states, accessing the dream world, understanding when spiritual presences are attempting to contact them, and venturing into the otherworld. That's not to say that other witches cannot do these things, but because the intuitive witch focuses on these abilities and utilizes these concepts in all their work, they naturally have an easier time doing it. Honing any skill means being able to perform it more efficiently and successfully, and the intuitive witch finds these parts of witchcraft a bit easier by virtue of sustained practice.

Intuitive witches are also a bit more self-sufficient. They work with the powers inside themselves rather than the correspondences outside the body, and so they don't necessarily need a large toolkit (though they can have one!) because they are their own power. Again, all witches have this ability, to some degree, as all witches hone the energy inside them to bring about change. But the intuitive witch works with that energy almost exclusively, and so if they don't have their tools, that's not a problem. Don't have a pendulum, for example? A simple writing tool and some paper will allow for spiritual contact.

Tools for the Intuitive Witch

TOOL	DESCRIPTION	PROPERTIES
Crystals	Crystals help channel and guide energy, no matter their individual correspondences.	Use crystals to help channel and build energy, to release energies placed into the stone, and to emit certain energies into space and person.
Drums	Drums come in all shapes, sizes, and materials; be mindful of the culture from which they come.	Drums, or the repetitive striking of them, enable achieving a trancelike or meditative state, which connects us better to the nonconscious self and to the spiritual side.
Ouija boards	Ouija boards feature letters and short words that allow spirits to communicate with us.	Ouija boards invite spirits in, but they also ask us to trust our intuition as the planchette moves across the board. Some say they're not moving the planchette, but others say they move it intuitively based on the subconscious instruction of spirits.
Pendulum	Pendulums are pointed stones on the end of a chain that move when entities are trying to communicate.	Each pendulum's energy is different depending on the crystal used for it. We can choose amethyst, aquamarine, celestite, classic quartz, and smoky quartz.
Planchettes	Planchettes are the tools used on Ouija boards to point out letters on the board and on which practitioners place their hands.	Planchettes allow the spirit to speak in more discernible ways, rather than relying on intuition and hoping it's the spirit.
Smoke or incense	Smoke or incense often comes from burning sacred herbs and resins.	This air element component of smoke or incense ushers out negativity, which is likely to come about when working with spirits and subtle energies in a space. Some resins and herbs help connect us to higher spirituality.

Focused Pathway 8
Psychic Witch

Psychic witchcraft is a broad category, as there are many types of psychic awareness. We can have psychic awareness by mediumship, or the ability to communicate with the dead, one of the most common types of psychic abilities and likely the one we think about when we think about being psychic. But there are many other activities considered psychic, such as astral projection, or the ability to roam about in spirit while the body lies dormant; the ability to speak to others via thoughts (telepathy); the ability to touch someone and gather thoughts, feelings, and history (psychometry); the ability to hear the dead (clairaudience); and—the one we all know—the ability to divine the future. All are vastly different from one another, but one thing is true. These psychic abilities rely on our mind-body connection and trust in our intuition. Your interests will guide you on this path, but we can start by honing psychic awareness skills in general and prepping the self for being in these charged spaces.

Our altars, in this regard, may feature mood boards or any personal items you think speak to that higher self. Maybe this includes imagery of places that speak to you spiritually, or ways of being, like someone meditating or doing yoga. If your goal is to speak to the inner or higher self, make sure that presence is felt on your altar.

Stones that reflect heightened spirituality or self-love are also ideal. Selenite, specifically peach selenite, connects us to the spiritual side and encourages confidence, healing, transformation, and love.

Include any symbols that speak to you spiritually as well. If an animal and its qualities symbolize those qualities you want in yourself, add that imagery (a wolf for courage, for instance). Colors can also add intention; purple corresponds to spirituality. But listen to your intuition when you think about what needs to be on your altar. You will feel the inner self "yay" or "nay" to items as you consider them.

GETTING STARTED (BEGINNER)

Getting started on this pathway may not be exciting at first, but the beginner's journey on this path has to be, first and foremost, safe. Whether we're working with inside energies that lurk in the unknown subconscious, or outside energies that lurk in our spaces, we're subject to a lot of not-so-ideal vibes and so must

focus on shielding and purifying spaces. This becomes more apparent when we realize that spiritual communication attempts may not end when we want them to. Outside entities can wish to communicate when the witch is "off duty." So, boundaries are needed.

Purification and Shielding

It's essential that psychic witches know how to protect themselves from intrusions, and a couple of ways to do so are to purify or cleanse the self and to shield the self. Cleansing the self is removing all the energetic residue that may unintentionally latch on to us from being in a spiritually or energetically intense space, and shielding the self means putting up a guard that helps protect us from absorbing that energy.

❦ Smoke Spell for Protection

Use this smoke spell before any psychic practices or spiritual communication to cleanse and protect the self. You can also use this spell when you want to build spiritual boundaries and need the confidence to do so (it's hard placing boundaries with ancestors when they want to communicate).

When to perform this spell:
Before any spiritual communication, meditation, or shadow work

Ingredients/tools:
Inscribing tool, such as a thorn, needle, quill, or nib
Large white pillar candle
5 thorns from a hawthorn tree
Dirt, enough to make a circle
Matches or a lighter
Dried oak and birch leaves and bark, finely ground together
Palm-size smoky quartz stone (placed on the altar for added protection
   or held as a necklace or in the pocket for protection)

1. Inscribe the word "safe" into the candle 7 times, one stacked on top of the other.

2. Below this, insert the thorns into the candle, spaced evenly around the circumference. They will stick out a bit.

3. Place your candle in the center of your altar or space and cast a circle around the candle with the dirt.

4. Light the candle and watch the flame's movements, allowing your vision to see "beyond" the flame. You'll likely focus on the flame's aura, the ring around the flame that holds a certain light. Chant lightly, "Safe and cleansed. The self, it mends. The spirit speaks and I'm here to listen, but then they slip into the distance."

5. Sprinkle your oak-birch mixture into the wax pool and allow the flame to burn it. These are protective and cleansing trees, respectively.

6. Carefully, so as not to disturb the wax pool, guide the candle around the body—taking note of the mind, heart center, and hands—to coat the skin with smoke from the flame and symbolically coat the body in these intentions. As you do, chant, "Mind the body, the body's mine, guarded from the spiritual side."

7. Place the candle back where it came from and envision a protective layer of energy around the self until you feel intuitively that it's set. This may feel like a sense of completion or calm, like the satisfaction you get from completing a task.

Enhancing Psychic Abilities

To build our psychic abilities, we can access the garden. There are plenty of herbs and plants* that correspond to enhanced psychic abilities by allowing us to fall into a stronger meditative state, or by opening the pathway to the spiritual realm. We can find these herbs in their dried form, meant to be burned, offered, or sprinkled, or in their ingestible tonic or tea form, meant to induce the tranquil mental state needed to open ourselves to psychic awareness.

*Safety Note: *Use only safe and ingestible herbal items made by reputable companies in doses deemed safe by medical communities and read the manufacturer's instructions carefully.*

❦ Peppermint Leaf Candle Dressing

We can make candles dressed in peppermint leaves so that no matter which psychic endeavor we wish to undergo, we have a tool ready to support the magic. Burn the candles as you would any candle, but note that these can be a bit messy.

When to perform this spell:

Monday, any time (3 p.m. or 10 p.m. are ideal)

Ingredients/tools:
Baking sheet
Parchment paper
1 cup (213 g) soy wax
Pine or sweetgrass essential oil (optional, see page 64)
5 white or purple chime candles
Dried peppermint leaves, preferably small leaves
Carrier oil of choice (optional, see page 64)

1. Line a baking sheet with parchment paper and have another piece of parchment nearby.

2. Heat the wax 10 to 15 minutes on medium heat on the stove so it melts completely, and then set aside to cool. The wax should be a bit cloudy when you work with it, which prevents it from being so hot that it melts the chime candles when poured onto them.

3. If desired, add the essential oil to the wax when it becomes cloudy until you like the scent.

4. Place the base of one chime candle on the parchment-lined baking sheet, holding the candle by the wick and at an angle that allows you to twist it as you pour.

5. Slowly, pour a small stream of melted wax onto the candle, rotating the candle deosil (clockwise) until the entire circumference is coated. It's okay if excess wax pools on the parchment.

6. Sprinkle or place your peppermint leaves on the candle's sides. The poured wax acts as glue. Place the coated candle on a clean piece of parchment and let it dry.

7. Repeat this process to coat the remaining 4 candles.

8. If desired, once the wax on the parchment begins to be of "mashed potato" consistency, use it to place a second coat on each candle.

9. If you prefer to use only an essential and carrier oil mixture to dress your candles, omit the wax and dress the candles only with the oil mixture and herbs. However, some do not like their candles feeling perpetually wet and messy, and so they use wax to "glue" the herbs to the candle.

Meditation

Meditation is a natural inclusion for the intuitive witch, because it's in that meditative space where we begin to have a deeper sense of the self, and the pathway to the spiritual side is open. There are different levels of meditation, beginner and intermediate, so we will start with beginner meditation to help us identify the more subtle parts of the self, including that coveted practice of being able to identify where in your body your spiritual energy sits. It's that spiritual energy that you infuse into your magic, and so you need to understand how to find it and move it in order to perform witchcraft.

❦ Meditation Spell: Finding Energy in the Body

It's hard to harness and send energy to different parts of the body if you've never really worked with that skill. But this skill is the basis for energy movement and manipulation in magic because it's how we move our intention, and the energy behind it, out of our body and into the ether to be manifested.

When to perform this spell:
Any day, any time

Ingredients/tools:
The self

1. Quiet the self and sit in a relaxed position and breathe. For this exercise, hyperfocus on the tip of the pinky finger on your dominant hand.

2. Focus on the finger and its tip alone. Envision it in your mind and attempt to feel any buzzing or movement in the tip. Perhaps your energy manifests as a slight heat. Give a look or feel to this energy. (Mine is always a black vibrating movement of shadows, buzzing back and forth within the finger. As I move my focus down to the knuckle, the energy moves with my focus, and I feel the heat and buzzing move in tandem.)

3. Slowly, make your way down to the base of the finger near the palm. (I feel and sense a buzzing drift in the direction of the other fingers as I attempt to move into them to reach their tips. If your energy wants to do this, let it.) Play around with this energy and continue to move it. In additional meditations, focus on another part of the body. No need to merge out of the meditation softly. Simply place the energy where you want it to stay.

4. For some (like me), this energy is going to sit right below the tip of the finger(s), lying in wait until you direct it to leave. It sits and it stews there, waiting for your word. When ready, it leaks into the tips of the fingers and seeps out of them. This movement out can look like ink dripping from a quill, or smoke coming out of the skin. (Mine looks more like thick ink—the color of which depends on the spell-work I am doing and my intention—that drips out and onto the floor.) This "ink" (energy) soaks into any candles, crystals, cards, or other tools being used. For others, this energy may need to be harnessed from the third eye, the heart, or any other space where it sits dormant. That's okay. We all hold our energy in different places.

5. Wherever the energy sits, hyperfocus on that area and send the energy to the finger-tips to move it out of the body.

6. Perform this spell as many times as you'd like, each time focusing on a small detail, such as the specific color of the energy or the way it moves around in the body and out of it

7. When you're finished with the activity, focus on your breathing and slowly open your eyes. Come back into the present.

INTERMEDIATE PSYCHIC WITCHCRAFT

Arguably, intermediate intuitive witchcraft is some of the hardest to do. You're tapping into the deepest parts of the self and attempting to contact the spiritual world to speak to that inner "you," ideally developing an almost natural skill. Messages and thoughts, wherever they're coming from, be it a spirit or the self, come almost immediately. There is a reason it's believed that this kind of witchcraft is hereditary or otherwise born into a person—developing it is difficult. But it can be done.

Extrasensory: The "Clair" Senses

Extrasensory perception, or ESP, is a kind of psychic awareness. Clairvoyance, in general, is the ability to divine future events, as well as glean information about someone or something by way of being in its presence or touching it. There are several types of "clair" abilities.

Clairvoyance is the ability to gain information through second sight, such as visions that pop up much like memories, whereas *clairaudience* is the ability to receive messages and information by hearing them, usually by way of entities. *Claircognizance* is the ability to just know information—it blossoms in the mind instantaneously after being in the presence of someone or something, or touching it. And *clairsentience* is the ability to gain insight by feelings. We may feel how another person feels, emotionally and physically.

Some say you can't make yourself "clair" anything. You're born with it. But intuitive witches know, much like other intuitive skills, you can harness that energy for these skills and develop them. And much like other intuitive skills, start by reading the subtle hints your mind, body, and spirit give you.

❧ Developing Clairvoyance

Use this spell to open yourself up to any clairvoyant skills. This spell appeals to the spiritual side to help open that pathway.

When to perform this spell:
Wednesday, at midnight, when the moon is waxing or full

Ingredients/tools:
Dish
Black sand or salt
3 purple chime or votive candles
Black salt
Matches or a lighter
Rosemary bundle
Abalone shell

1. Fill the dish with black sand or salt. Arrange the candles in the dish to form a triangle and so they are stable. Around the dish, place a circle of black salt.

2. Light the rosemary bundle. With these flames, as you stand, begin coating the self with the smoke, moving from around the feet up toward the top of the head.

3. As you wrap around the feet, state, "The base of self levitates. I reach the otherworldly state."

4. As you move toward the hips and waist, say, "The smoke is the fog through which spirits venture. Around the legs and toward the center."

5. Coming up to the heart, state, "The heart's the gate where messages arise. They pierce the veil of midnight's sky."

6. When you reach your third eye, share, "From heart's center, the mind's eye reads. Now, I sense spirit's wants and needs."

7. As you come to the top of the head, whisper, "Out of crown, the spiritual peak. Through my person, the spiritual speaks."

8. Put the bundle on the abalone shell and stand again, placing your palms at your sides, facing outward, open to what's in front of you. Focus on your breath. If you'd like, sit and place your hands on your knees, palms facing upward. Stand, or sit, here for some time, envisioning yourself absorbing energy like a beacon.

9. Let the candles burn through. Extinguish the rosemary bundle, if you'd like.

THE HIGHER SELF

There are many interpretations of the self, depending on the psychological approach used. It gets a bit muddy when discussing this because the interpretation truly depends on who you ask and a bit of context. For our purposes, we'll talk about three levels of self: the basic self, the conscious self, and the higher self.

The *basic self,* ourselves at base line, is what we're born with, and it includes parts of the self that govern basic needs as well as basic emotions not yet regulated by higher thinking. This is the self that holds almost childlike desires and wants, but it's also the self that understands survivability and what's needed to maintain that. It's the self that holds instincts.

Then, there's the *conscious self,* the self we are currently. This self can be divided, depending on the lens you're using, into who we are individually, alongside close relationships, among society, and so on. It could also be broken down into how we view and value ourselves, and more. Though some call this the conscious self, because it's the self we operate with day to day, we can see that some aspects of this self delve deeper than just conscious understandings of who we are, what we look like, what we enjoy, and how we are.

Then, there's the *higher self,* who operates with a spiritual wisdom, the foresight, and an emotional intelligence that we, in our current state, strive to be. It's the self that can regulate the needs of the basic self and put them in context to make more sense. It's the part of us that can approach the current conscious self with understanding from the unconscious self to grow.

You may believe the higher self lies latent in the mind, body, and spirit, waiting for us to tap into it. Or, maybe you believe the higher self is an ideal self we achieve through growth in the current state, usually brought about by spiritual guidance and higher-order thinking. Or, maybe your ideas are somewhere in the middle. What matters is that we can work with this imagery to better understand the self.

❧ Meeting the Higher Self: A Meditation

This meditation involves venturing into the spiritual realm to meet the higher self as we envision it and, perhaps, gain a bit of wisdom through symbols or spiritual messages in the process.

When to perform this spell:
Any day (Monday is ideal)

Ingredients/tools:
Light pink, orange, yellow, white, and green pillar candles,
   the number of candles is up to you
Coconut oil mixed with dried willow leaf or bark
   (rosemary can substitute)
Matches or a lighter

1. Anoint your candles with the oil mixture.

2. Light your candles and situate them in front of you. Each color offers a specific correspondence: healing and the inner self (light pink), courage (orange), communication (yellow), purity and spiritual connection (white), and foundation (green).

3. Face the northern direction and begin breathing slowly. Focus on your breath and how it inhabits your being, where it sits in the body. Attempt to move it from the chest to the belly and back again to practice identifying where it is at any given moment. When you begin the meditation, place this breath in the chest.

4. Place your hands on your thighs or knees for added foundation. In your mind's eye, envision yourself at a hedge covered by ivy, brambles, berries, and mosses. Birds flutter near the iron gate and squirrels search the ground for acorns. The gate cuts through tall, ancestral trees, growing around the gate to accommodate it. Unlike other gates, this one is spiritual and the earth is okay with its presence. You walk along this hedge, picking a blackberry and nibbling on it.

As you pick it, you hear the rustling of the bush as it bends to your picking and then snaps back to its original position. The wind picks up, and your clothes dance. You go to pick another berry and notice the gate latch is open. It wavers a little in the wind, making a light noise from the hinges. You push it a little to see if it welcomes you, and it does, opening with ease. The roots of the oak and the tendrils of moss slink back to let the gate open. You begin walking down the dirt pathway.

The wind becomes more intense, whipping around the tall trees. It's a forested area, but it's not dense. You can hear the soil move underneath your feet. The dusk's sun sinks into your skin.

You reach an opening where the grasses are tall and bending to the wind. The clouds are a bit pink and orange, hiding the sun and then exposing it all at once. It's a liminal space, and you call upon this higher self to join you, to meet you and guide you. This is a personal call, not a general invocation. It should come from inside and from intuition. State your call out loud in this meditation. You will begin to feel a presence behind you as the wind brings this being to you.

This being has an ethereal look, with a soft white ambience as an aura. The hair flips around in the wind, as do the clothes, but the face is fixed on you with a loving smile. A knowing one. This being waits patiently for you to begin asking for guidance or sharing your story.

5. You can simply meet this person and venture back outward, or stay and ask for assistance. Either way, when you're done, give your thanks and turn back the way you came in, maybe nibbling a berry as you venture outward.

Focused Pathway 9
Cosmic Witch

We may not see immediately how the cosmic witch, or the witch who focuses on celestial bodies and events, may fit with intuitive spellwork at first. But when we think of intuition and working with the spiritual side, be it of ourselves or another realm, we can see better how this fits. After all, spirituality is understanding there is something bigger than ourselves at play, and what's the ultimate thing bigger than ourselves . . . the cosmos. The cosmos hold mysteries of creation, of being, of spiritual energy or divine beings. It's these mysteries that the human condition—and the witch, specifically—seeks to understand. It makes sense that we may look to the cosmos for spiritual resources on these human questions.

GETTING STARTED (BEGINNER)

To begin on this path, cosmically, we look closer to home. The sun and moon are often the focus of the beginner astro witch, and we can use these two celestial bodies as umbrella correspondences. Whereas the planets will provide more specific intentions, the sun and moon offer generalized intentions. Their corresponding days are Sunday and Monday, respectively.

☉ The Sun

The sun embodies positivity and abundance, strength, money, fame, and reaching goals, be they business or personal, leadership and prosperity. It is represented in colors of yellow, orange, gold, and copper, and in rich silken textiles and herbs and plants of the same colors and intentions. In shadow work or healing work, the sun offers rebirth and rejuvenation, vitality and emotional energy as well as physical. This goes back to Celtic days, when we honored the sun during Samhain, on the brink of winter, as its departure meant it was time for winter's darkness, which symbolized reflection, silence, and fortitude.

☾ The Moon

The moon's intentions are many: psychic and lucid dream abilities, divination, subconscious states and meditation, sleep, healing, and more. These are generally separated into the understandings of the Triple Goddess in each of her "states." We're hard-pressed to venture into moon magic without references to the Triple Goddess, or at least the phases and what they mean.

Triple Goddess image of three moons.

🌒 **Maiden:** This is the moon in her *waxing state.* We use this time for rebirth, sexuality, bravery and courage, beginning difficult challenges, and harnessing our focus.

🌕 **Mother:** This is the moon in her *full state.* This version corresponds to full power and full potential, comfort and care, guidance, protection, and love.

🌘 **Crone:** The crone state is symbolized by the moon in its *waning state.* The crone symbolizes the apathy of life and the chaos that includes, but it also symbolizes tough love, wisdom, death as a cycle of life, and ancestral connection.

USING THE PLANETS AND THEIR QUALITIES

As beginners, we can use the planets, their correspondences, and symbols in our magic. Each planet has a variety of intentions, so even the most specific spellwork has a planet that can relate to the topic at hand. You'll also begin to notice that planets have individual correspondences beyond days. Herbs, colors, elements, and directions also relate to the planets. And so, we begin to see the interconnectedness between types of witches when we look at the planets and what they rule.

♂ Mars

Mars corresponds to passion, bravery, impulsiveness, motivation, and fortitude. We can use the waxing moon or the sun to add to these intentions. In addition, we would perform this magic on Tuesday, and we could inscribe the symbol in any candles or as part of any sigils. Herbs include black pepper, cactus, chile peppers, coriander, pine, and thistle. Colors are red, orange, brown, and black. Mars is part of the fire element and the southern direction is as an additional Mars correspondence.

☿ Mercury

Mercury is the planet of communication, but it also relates to mental strength, creativity, and inspiration. We would perform this magic on Wednesdays. It is a very air-focused planet, and so we might use that element in our spells as well as its corresponding eastern direction. Herbs that correspond to Mercury include clover, fennel, fern, lavender, lemon balm, lemon verbena, and mint. Yellow, purple, and orange are its corresponding colors.

♃ Jupiter

Jupiter is the planet for business, as it pertains to leadership and prosperity, so it may be used with the sun for money-related pursuits. However, it's also the planet of healing and may be used in tandem with the moon. We would perform our magic on Thursdays to correspond to this planet. Herbal correspondences include maple, meadowsweet, nutmeg, and oak. Use blues, greens, and purples as color correspondences, and sit in the southern direction for business-related endeavors; use east for healing. Because of Jupiter's correspondences, this planet relates to both the fire and water elements, and the directions best used would be south and east.

♀ Venus

Venus is known as the planet of love, self-love, fertility, sex, confidence, beauty, and relationships, but we can use this planet as a correspondence in any magic that pertains to a partner or friend to whom the magic relates. The planet's color correspondences are pink, red, and blue. Let the nature of the spell determine the direction you use. Healing spells concerning a break-up may use the southern (endings) or eastern directions (new beginnings), for instance. Fridays correspond to Venus, and because of its subject matter, Venus can appeal to the water or fire element. Corresponding plants include apple leaves and blossoms, coriander, daisy, hawthorn, primrose, rose, and vanilla.

♄ Saturn

Saturn is the go-to planet for banishing, and its corresponding day is Saturday (naturally). We use black colors for this work with Saturn. Because banishing can relate to any topic, the spellwork will guide the element and the direction. For instance, spellwork pertaining to banishing negative thoughts would relate to the air element and therefore correspond to the eastern direction. Plant correspondences include horsetail.

♅ Uranus

Uranus relates to changes, problems, or situations. We might use this planet and its correspondences to help guide us through these changes, and we may pair it with another planet to get more specific. We may pair Uranus with Venus, for example, if the changes deal with love. Uranus's day is also Wednesday, and it corresponds with bright blue colors. Plant correspondences include blue flowers and herbs, such as borage, cornflower, and the heartfelt pansy. Uranus relates to the air element (east).

♆ Neptune

Neptune's day is also Friday. The planet corresponds with dreams, spiritual heightening, strengthening intuitive skills, and inspiration. This all intuitively makes sense because Neptune is a watery planet, the element most associated with emotion and feeling, which naturally also relates to love (Venus), Friday's correspondence. Any watery plants, such as iris, kelp, lotus, and seaweed, relate to this planet. The colors blue, purple, and white correspond to Neptune.

♇ Pluto

Pluto can be associated with Saturn, and often is because of its nature to ward off obstacles and banish for the sake of renewal. Saturday is its corresponding day. It also works with Uranus because it offers transformation. It makes sense, then, that we would use black as a color correspondence to Pluto. Pluto relates to the southern direction and the element of fire for its banishing properties, but it may also relate to air because of its tendency to create change and bring about rebirth. Related plants include hollyhock, pansy, and petunia.

☘ Sun Vitality Tea Spell

To sip sun magic, we can craft sun tea. This tea is made in a clear glass vessel left to meld in the sun on a hot summer's day. Use any tea you like, but I prefer black teas because they offer a protective quality, like the sun.

When to perform this spell:
Sunday, at noon

Ingredients/tools:
One 16- to 32-ounce (475- to 950-ml) glass vessel
¼ cup (8 g) loose black tea
3 whole cloves
1 tablespoon dried hibiscus
¼ teaspoon ground cinnamon
½ teaspoon orange extract
Aluminum foil, enough to cover the top of the
    vessel and wrap around the rim
Cheesecloth
Rubber band

1. Fill a 16- to 32-ounce (475- to 950-ml) glass vessel nearly to the top with water and add the tea, cloves, hibiscus, cinnamon, and orange extract. Stir deosil (clockwise) to blend.

2. Cover the vessel with aluminum foil and place it in a sunny spot for at least 4 hours.

3. Every so often, remove the foil and stir the tea, enchanting it by stating as you stir 3 times around, deosil (clockwise), "Infused with vitality. Enhanced longevity. Increased energy by round of three."

4. Take a sip occasionally to taste the strength of the tea, adding additional ingredients as you wish.

5. When ready, remove the aluminum foil and replace it with cheesecloth secured with a rubber band. Strain the mixture. Alternatively, use a French press or a fine-mesh sieve, if you prefer.

Days of the Week

Planets also rule over the days of the week, as we learned from their descriptions, and so we can add even more correspondence by using those designated days to determine the timing of our spells. Naturally, this means choosing the most relevant day, but we can go a bit further than just that. Witches can work with the same intention but on different days to bring about different elements of change. For instance, in a love spell, we may use Monday to tap into dormant feelings or hidden desires, Wednesday to communicate those feelings, and Friday to strengthen our attachments and conscious connection to our partners. Although we could do the entire spell in one day, it makes sense to spread it out to add the correspondences of the different days and their corresponding planetary rulers.

☿Mercury Communication Spell

This spell will be personal, as the purpose behind needing to communicate differs, and the emotions do, too. The following is a "communication charm" you can personalize if you'd like to make it more specific to your situation.

When to perform this spell:
Wednesdays, at noon

Ingredients/tools:
Inscribing tool, such as a thorn or needle
2 pillar candles, either yellow or orange
Full moon or waxing moon water (water that sat
   in the moonlight during either of these phases)
Dish
Salt or sand
Twine
Any personalized items from the person you want to contact
Symbols for love, such as a rose quartz or roses, or symbols for friendship,
   such pink colors, daisies, or zinnias (optional)
Matches or a lighter
Goose feather

1. Inscribe the symbol for mercury into the candles (see page 143).

2. Rub moon water into this symbol on both candles.

3. Cover the bottom of a dish with enough salt or sand to hold the candles securely.

4. Tie the candles together with a bit of twine, ideally in the middle. Place them in the salt or sand, making sure they're steady and stable.

5. Inscribe the initials of the person to whom you wish to speak in one candle, and your initials in the other. If you have anything to represent the other person, place the item near their candle.

6. If you like, and depending on the relationship, place a rose quartz (partners, spouses) near the candle or a daisy (friends).

7. Light your candle first, and then the other. With a goose feather, waft the smoke and play with the flame to move the energies upward, as the air element offers communication and movement. As you do this, state, "Wings of the bird who sounded the warning, all while the dogs had slept. I ask you to touch the shoulder of [name of person] to remind them of bonds that need to be kept."

8. Let the candles burn and envision messages or phone calls coming through. Take note of the candles and of which burns first, which sparks the twine, and so on. These are indicators of the state of that relationship. Interpret intuitively.

Intermediate Cosmic Witchcraft

For intermediate cosmos magic, we look beyond the celestial bodies closest to us and venture into how the other planets can charge and otherwise affect our tools, the planetary movements and their interactions with one another, and cosmic events, like eclipses. All these are studied heavily by those who delve deep into the nuances of astrology and astronomy, including how they affect us on a daily basis and how we can harness that interaction between the self and the cosmos to create magic.

Individual astrological signs play a role here; they, too, have planetary rulers. And so, if we're a Virgo (ruled by Mercury), we may inscribe our planetary symbol into a blue candle to ease feelings of stress and evince feelings of tranquility. At this stage, we look at the interconnectedness of the cosmos with the nature witch, as each planet and astrological sign fits with an element that speaks not only to the nature of those under that astrological sign, but also to what they may want to focus on for spiritual equilibrium. For instance, a Virgo may be part of the earth element, which governs objectivity and rational thinking. But for the Virgo, whose nature is to be highly detail oriented and, perhaps, a bit high strung, the earth element is less a description of the person but more so an indicator of what they need to find their equilibrium.

Astrological Signs and Their Correspondences

SIGN	BIRTH DATES	PLANET	ELEMENT
♈︎ Aries	March 21–April 19	♂ Mars	△ Fire
♉︎ Taurus	April 20–May 20	♀ Venus	▽ Earth
♊︎ Gemini	May 21–June 21	☿ Mercury	△ Air
♋︎ Cancer	June 22–July 22	☽ Moon	▽ Water
♌︎ Leo	July 23–August 22	☉ Sun	△ Fire
♍︎ Virgo	August 23–September 22	☿ Mercury	▽ Earth
♎︎ Libra	September 23–October 23	♀ Venus	△ Air
♏︎ Scorpio	October 24–November 21	♇ Pluto	▽ Water
♐︎ Sagittarius	November 22–December 21	♃ Jupiter	△ Fire
♑︎ Capricorn	December 22–January 19	♄ Saturn	▽ Earth
♒︎ Aquarius	January 20–February 18	♅ Uranus	△ Air
♓︎ Pisces	February 19–March 20	♆ Neptune	▽ Water

Celestial Charging

Just like the sun and moon, the other celestial bodies can charge our tools, waters, and more. We can do this several ways: adding herbal correspondences to those planets, setting the tools out when the planet is clearly visible, or by choosing the day associated with the planet to charge the items.

❧ Saturn Spell for Charging Banishing Stones

Use this charm when you want to banish negative feelings. Here, we're charging a stone with the energy of Saturn's day (Saturday) and the moon for optimum celestial correspondence.

When to perform this spell:
Saturday, any time (6 p.m. or 10 p.m. are ideal)

Ingredients/tools:
3 pieces ½-inch (12-mm)-thick ribbon or textile of black and purple
(any ratio will do: two purple and one black, for instance)
Iron nail
Black candle
Apache stone charged in waning moon water
Matches or a lighter

1. At one end of each of your colored ribbons or textiles, draw the symbol for Saturn with the nail (see page 144).

2. Light the candle and use its wax to secure the three ribbons, on the ends without the symbols, to the Apache stone.

3. Wrap the ribbons around the stone at the same time. As you do, state, "The winds went south, and so, too, did I. I banish the tar that drowns me. The heaviness that sits in the chest, this omits. As these threads make their way around me."

4. Repeat the charm until the threads are wrapped all around the stone.

5. When done, place the stone under the waning moon until it is a new moon. The stone is now charged by the moon and the day for added power in banishing.

Combining Your Celestial Magic

Now that we see how many correspondences intertwine, we can begin connecting them, adding them together. We can, for instance, combine our astrological sign, as well as the sign of others who play a role in our spellwork (for love, it may be our partner, or for business, it may be our boss) with the astrological sign of a planet that relates. These signs, then, may be featured on a colored candle corresponding to the element we need to invoke. To this, we can provide a day that corresponds to the planets we may wish to invoke, and so on. There is much to take in, and many options. Although there is no right or wrong grouping of correspondences, we want to consider as many as possible.

We may, for instance, want to communicate with another, and so we may use Mercury as insight into the day and symbol to use. But we may also want to use the moon as a symbol if, instead, it is secrets we want to share, or Neptune if what we wish to communicate is difficult to talk about. All three could be used. But you can begin to see how using all three really helps specify the intention.

❦ Celestial Spell for Healing

We can use the powers of Neptune, Uranus, Pluto, and the Moon for a more complex spell to let our intuition guide us through unforeseen and painful changes so that we can heal. In this spell, we combine the celestial bodies associated with healing, transformation, emotion, and intuition, as well as our own cosmic self, to find a path out of the pain.

When to perform this spell:
Thursday, 8 p.m.

Ingredients/tools:
Rose quartz point, used as an inscription tool
Five candles: silver, black, purple, blue, white
Matches or a lighter

1. With the point of your rose quartz stone, draw the following cosmic symbols into their respective candles: Inscribe the moon symbol into the silver candle; the Pluto symbol into the black candle; the Uranus symbol into the purple candle; and the Neptune symbol in the blue candle (see pages 142–145). For the white candle, write your name or use your astrological sign's symbol (see page 151).

2. Place the candles around the white one in the following directions: the blue candle (Neptune) in the western direction; the black candle (Pluto) in the southern direction; the purple candle (Uranus) in the eastern direction; and the silver candle (Moon) in the northern direction.

3. Light the silver Moon candle first, and use it to light the purple Uranus candle. As you do, state, "Mother Moon and Father Earth guide the intuition, for change has come and it's unwanted, and I'm needing a solution."

4. Use the purple Uranus candle to light the black Pluto candle. While doing this, say, "Transformation takes the reins, but the journey meets no hardship. I come upon the other side as wise and yet unhardened."

5. Use the black Pluto candle to light the blue Neptune candle and while doing so, state, "As dark as sky when night's arrived, I look to the celestial. I will heal. I will feel. A weight will lift. Thanks to the cosmic ancestral."

6. Use the Neptune candle, holding the energies from each candle before it, to light your own white candle in the middle. Repeat, " I will heal. I will feel. Weight will lift. Thanks to the cosmic ancestral."

7. Let the candles burn until they extinguish.

Focused Pathway 10
Shadow Witch

Shadow witchcraft is a loaded term. It's tossed around during autumn and winter, when the seasons tend to go dormant and people venture inside from the cold. In this reclusive state, we tend to reflect on the self and look at patterns of behavior and habits of mind that tend to harm or hinder us more than help us.

But what is shadow witchcraft? To start, we have to understand what the shadow self is, a concept outlined by psychologist Carl Jung. The shadow self is the part(s) of the self we hide or otherwise temper. This part includes negative traits and habits and parts of the self we know are socially unacceptable. But the shadows include much more than that; they are memories and past experiences that act as a filter or lens, and we use that lens to view the world and interpret the actions and intentions of others and of the self. The shadows also includes basic desires that aren't quite molded by context or regulated by emotions, or those that are animalistic—anger, jealousy, revenge, sex, and so on.

When we become aware of the shadow self and try to integrate it into who we are currently, we achieve enlightenment and understanding. The shadow witch uses these understandings in spells related to finding and speaking to the shadow, unearthing repressed feelings and thoughts, accepting that side of the self, and integrating it into an overall understanding of the self. As you can imagine, that's no small undertaking.

GETTING STARTED (BEGINNER)

Shadow magic does have a place to begin, but it is one of the more intermediate practices of the craft because the stakes are high. After all, we're working with residues of the past and present, the lenses we use to perceive the world around us and the people in it, the habits and human natures that make us fallible, faulty, and fickle. It's not a quick undertaking. In fact, any journey into the shadows is a dangerous one, especially for those with anxiety and depression. We may tap into traumas, trigger ourselves, impact our mental wellness, and more. Shadow work requires strong intuition: intuition on when it's okay to explore a sensitive topic; intuition on when we should stop venturing into a memory.

The sense of self and our subtle energies needs to be strong before we engage, and so body scans and work on developing intuition is recommended before beginning shadow work.

Be mindful: We can conjure false memories if we try to venture into the past to remember events. And we can confuse these memories with repressed memories and believe they are real. This is another reason shadow work is dangerous; we can cause more harm than good to our psyche. Some journeys are best done with the guidance of professionals and modern medicine, and that is okay. We can support our journeys, but we don't want to make them worse. Before delving into your shadows, ask yourself whether it will do more harm than good, and listen to your intuition.

Shadow Magic

Shadow magic can take many forms, from meditating in a safe space, incorporating restful yoga poses into spells, or performing banishing spells to get rid of bad habits. The form depends on our goal. The best place to start is to open yourself up to the shadows, so you can see them through an objective lens rather than an emotionally charged one.

⚘ Spell for Opening the Shadows

This spell simply asks that when emotions or memories trigger intense or deep feelings, we step back and gain insight from the higher self on what's truly going on. Although we're not all psychologists, we can begin to piece together the "whys" of our actions by looking at them objectively.

When to perform this spell:
Friday or Saturday, any time

Ingredients/tools:
Baking sheet
Parchment paper
Dried thyme, eucalyptus, or rosemary
Dried roses
5 candles, either blue or black
Evening primrose carrier oil infused with smoky quartz
5 candleholders, to hold the candles you've chosen
Gray salt
Selenite sphere

1. Line a baking sheet with parchment paper.

2. On the prepared baking sheet combine the herb and roses.

3. Using gloves, coat the candles with the oil and roll them in the herb and rose mixture.

4. Place the candles in candleholders and arrange them in a circle.

5. With the salt, craft a circle to connect each candle.

6. Hold your selenite sphere above the candles and, moving deosil (clockwise), begin building speed as you rotate your hand around the circumference of the circle.

7. Slowly move your hand upward, forming a cone shape (think of it as an inverted tornado) as you go.

8. Let your breath match the increase of speed in the hand. As you move your hand upward, the breath gets heavier, faster. This is you building power.

9. As you exhale, envision the breath getting taken in by the force and movement of the hand. In essence, your breath is getting "sucked into" this tornado.

10.   As you reach the top, whisper:

> "I traipse across the hedge and open the iron gate.
> I reach inward to shadows long since built.
> Tell me. Speak your name.
> Come through the brambles and share the tales that solidified you to me.
> And in this space of safety and care, you can speak right through me."

11.   If the shadow wishes to speak at this moment, you may feel some new, impulsive, or otherwise "out-of-place" emotions, which may come as a surprise. This is the shadow speaking in feelings. Are there memories associated with these feelings? Feelings, like a quickened heartbeat? Take note of anything you experience. If there is nothing, that's okay; we're merely opening to the shadow and giving it space.

12.   Let the candles burn through. Hold this selenite sphere when you attempt to speak to the shadow self again, as it holds this power and corresponds now to this opening spell.

INTERMEDIATE SHADOW WITCHCRAFT

Intermediate shadow work may mean venturing further into the shadows to meet the nuances of self, with more memories, more hidden negative feelings or resentments. The shadow self is, after all, as complex as the conscious self. But in doing this work, we find that the shadow self may feel a bit exposed, and we can show a bit of gratitude for its hard work.

Self-Magic

At the heart of shadow work is a healing of the self. Ultimately, we want to use this magic to reach some sort of peace or enlightenment by way of acknowledging and working through, or at least accepting, our shadows. This healing may be quick confidence affirmations while holding a stone, or elaborate healing incantations wherein we ask to meet our higher self. No matter what they are, the goal is to take care of the self.

❦ The Shadow Bind: A Coming Together of Selves

Use this spell to acknowledge and honor the shadow as part of the self. If this act feels like a "burden" rather than a moment of "self-help" and compassion toward the self, don't perform the spell.

When to perform this spell:
Thursday, at dusk

Ingredients/tools:
Dish
Salt or sand
White pillar candle
Black pillar candle
Thread, preferably white, purple, or brown
Matches or a lighter

1. Cover the bottom of the dish with enough salt or sand to hold the candles securely.

2. Gather the candles and tie them together using the thread. Wrap the thread around the candles, deosil (clockwise), 9 times. Then, place the candles in the dish, making sure they're sturdy and stable.

3. Light the candles and, as they both burn together, their waxes mingling until they have burned completely through, state:

> "The journey is mine but also yours,
> the hand that guides my thoughts.
> I venture inward to save the self that feels like I forgot.
> A hearty bind, through life, we hold, and in it is my faith
> that through this tether, both together, we heal in our own ways."

Ritual Magic

Rituals are a bit more involved than average spells. They are likely going to "call the corners," a ritual that involves asking the elements to join you and protect you, as well add their power to yours, if they want to. A ritual may also involve casting a protective circle. Although circles are always recommended, or at least some sort of protection, circle castings offer an outright statement that the space is open but protected, and that nothing but what's desired can cross through. And although rituals may be more expected of the shadow witch who is working with more high-stakes spells, these rituals are very common in any spellwork wherein the witch wants to make sure they have protection, blessings, and support.

❧ Calling the Corners

Use this ritual when you want to ask the elements to assist you in your spellwork, especially hard work where spiritual support is nice to have. As we learned in chapter 4, each element corresponds to helpful facets of the self. Water corresponds to opening emotions; fire gives us the bravery to do so; earth offers grounding; and air brings comfort in change. And so it makes sense that when performing emotionally intense spellwork, we seek out the elements to bring their best traits forward to help. You're not limited to shadow work when calling the corners. Do this ritual with any spell for which you need additional power and spiritual support.

When to perform this spell:
Immediately before performing a spell

Ingredients/tools:
Salt
Offerings of choice
Altar dish
Oil of choice
Matches or a lighter
Altar candle
Smoke cleansing bundle of choice
Additional salts, herbs, or stones of choice

1. With the salt, craft a protective circle wherever you.

2. Place any offerings along the circle in the appropriate directions for the elements (west: water; south: fire; east: air; north: earth).

3. Situate yourself in a calming space in front of or, depending on the size of your circle, within the circle. Quietly, chant the following:

    "The earth breeds its bounty, the seeds are sown,
    and as above, so below.
    The air will rise, it skirts and blows,
    and as above, so below.
    The fire breathes, its embers glow,
    and as above, so below.
    The water's tides, they ebb and flow,
    and as above, so below."

4. Fill an altar dish with oil. Face west, holding the dish of oil toward the sky, and state, "West, the keeper of tides, the enabler of growth, the ruler of emotions and psychical flow, I invoke you."

5. Light the altar candle. Face south, holding the candle toward the sky, and state, "South, the keeper of warmth and of fire, and flame of bravery, abundance, prosperity, and fame, I invoke you."

6. Light the smoke cleansing bundle and, holding it, face east and state, "East, the wind child, the mother of breath, the bringer of beginnings after duress, I invoke you."

7. While holding the salts, herbs, or stones, face north and state, "North, the pillar of fertility and strength, of grounding the center and renewing my faith, I invoke you."

8. If you are not there now, step into the middle of the circle to invoke Spirit. Raise your hands high and state:

    "I invoke the ether,
    the ancestral divine,
    the spiritual keeper
    of the secrets of life.
    What fosters beyond,
    what conjures below,
    I invoke the spirit
    for whom this circle's bestowed."

9. Now, perform any spellwork for which you wanted or needed the added power of the elements. Think of calling the corners as the bread to a sandwich. It surrounds the main focus: the spell.

10. When you're finished with your spellwork, close the circle by stating:

> "I close this circle, the spell has ceased.
> It's time to dance, to play, to feast.
> Water, earth, smoke, and flame,
> you may return from whence you came.
> Entities, spirits, any beings now tethered,
> I cast you out of this space unfettered.
> My sisters, my ancestors, my limbs are alighted,
> your spirits run through me; I leave you ignited."

Dark Moon Magic

The moon symbolizes secrets, as the tarot will tell you. It symbolizes the sub-conscious and deeply held feelings. It's also the ruler of tides, and so it's directly linked to the element of water, which also corresponds to emotions, dreams, the subconscious, intuition, divination, and psychic abilities. Because of this, we look to the moon, particularly in her "dark" or crone, state for support in shadow work.

Shadow work, as we've explored, is the work we do in the winter months, as the earth goes dormant and returns to itself. It's a time of solitude and reflection, of taking stock and getting rid of what does not offer us much. As the earth does this, we do, too, performing spells for help on self-reflection, healing, working through or honoring anger, banishing habits or negativity from our lives (be they people or spirits or neither), and so on.

❧ Drawing Down the Moon

The ritual of Drawing Down the Moon comes from *The Grimoire of Lady Sheba*, a book from 1972, and Janet and Stewart Farrar's book *Eight Sabbats for Witches* (1981). Although it may not be the ancient ritual we think it is, the act of possession or being taken by a deity, who is controlling the body, is an antiquated practice.

Drawing down the moon is not an easy feat, and it is not for the faint of heart. Instead of invoking the moon for her support and guidance, the act of "drawing down" is a possessive act, asking the moon deity of your choice to inhabit the body and to guide thoughts by controlling or influencing them. There are many rituals to teach you how to draw down the moon, some more rigid and technical depending on your belief system (Wicca, for instance), or who you ask. Like any common ritual, it's been revised and recanted many times over, altered to fit personal tastes and more. If anyone tells you there is a "right" way to draw down the moon, they are erroneous.

Some rituals include two people, one to guide and one to be "possessed"; some include certain structures and only higher members of a group. For the ritual, remember these three things:

1.   Craft a place of protection and power.
2.   Be explicit about what you are asking the deity to do.
3.   Provide some sort of offering as thanks.

All else will find a place. If you are going about this ritual alone, I suggest using some sort of trance music or drums to help usher you out of the experience, which is what the additional person would have done (as well as other tasks).

When to perform this spell:
Monday, at midnight when the moon is waning

Ingredients/tools:
Black salt
Offerings of feathers, moonstones, smoky quartz,
   rose quartz, regular quartz
Pad and paper
Thick gray pillar candle
All moon waters: waxing, full, waning
Matches or a lighter
Trance music (optional)

1.   Sit in the western direction and create a black salt circle around you (ideally), or your altar space.
2.   Place your offerings in the middle of the circle, as well the pad and paper. Turn on any music, if you'd like.
3.   Anoint your candle with the waters, in order from maiden to mother to crone (see page 142), starting from the middle of the candle and working your way down, and then starting from the middle and working your way up, rotating the candle deosil (clockwise) as you go.
4.   Place the candle in the center of the circle and light it.
5.   Make yourself comfortable and close your eyes. Raise your palms. Keep breathing, slow, steady, trancelike breaths. When you feel ready, begin chanting, "These earthen veins take mother's name."
6.   Chant until you feel a warm sensation in your body. Open your eyes and stare into the candle's flame. Repeat the chant, but gradually louder, raising your hands higher as you increase your volume. Close your eyes. The trick to this spell is staying

completely focused on the incantation below while hyperfocusing on the body, envisioning that warm sensation floating along the bloodline and into each appendage. State:

> "In heathen tongues, I searched the sun,
> I crawled and went to find her.
> I stumbled in darkness, alone in its harshness
> 'till I saw mother standing tall, her phases right beside her.
> Come into me, breathe from the lungs
> that, in time and age, will pass.
> Mix the blood with conjured soul,
> that, upon my death, will last.
> I take you in. I feed you.
> I take you in. I feed you.
> I take you in. I feed you.
> I act as the vessel."

7. Repeat the last line as many times as necessary. Envision gray tendrils of smoke arising from the mouth and venturing outward. Focus on the flame to see if any movement takes place.

8. From here, sit with yourself, deep in the depths of the chest. Envision yourself just as you're sitting, but in the body. Take hold of the pen and prepare to write, closing your eyes as you do. You may be inclined to write certain words or draw symbols. Record anything that comes to the mind on the paper.

9. When finished, close the spell by stating:

> "From the chest to mother's nest,
> the moon, in all her phases,
> ventures on and takes her blood,
> my own will now replace it.
> In the veins, the deepest drip,
> she slips through the fingers and leaves,
> takes shelter in the tides of night,
> and conjures a restful sleep.
> I release the conjure.
> I am myself.
> No entities will replace her.
> This is my vessel."

10. Let the candle extinguish and breathe slowly to ease back into the self. Focus on your breathing.

CHAPTER 7

ECLECTIC & NICHE WITCHES

By now, we've likely identified many facets of witchcraft you'd like to incorporate into your practice. Many witches pick and pull from different types of witchcraft, add spellwork based on personal connections to regions or lineage, toss in a bit of lore that interests them, and try out some inclusions because, well, why not? Then, we notice there are parts of different types of witchcraft that seem essential to working spells. Little bits that, depending on our understanding of how, exactly, things get manifested or how we connect to spirits, make sense for us to add to our practice. Understanding where the energy sits in the body in order to move it requires a bit of intuitive witchcraft practice. Maybe hearth spells fit your interests and lifestyle, but you like the idea of starting a garden and working with old plant lore and weather spells. Well then, welcome to eclectic witchcraft.

We can argue that, in contemporary times, witchcraft practices often include combinations of the different types we've covered in this book. And, as we talked about in chapter 3, as time passes, the witchcraft present in regions and in traditions melds based on generational needs, resource availability, and so on. Essentially, the craft evolves and changes for a variety of reasons. As a result, we can consider a good portion of witchcraft practiced today to be eclectic, or stemming from a variety of beliefs and traditions.

This is why we end our book with this chapter and talk about the inherent issues of labelling our witchcraft. Determining "types" of witchcraft is helpful in breaking down and clarifying the abstract and countless approaches to this ancient practice. If we didn't organize it all a bit, the amount of information and ideas presented would be overwhelming, especially for a beginner. However, like many things, it's not ideal to pigeonhole ourselves into a particular pathway because so many facets of the self are part of this choice: who we are at any given time, where we live, what we're interested in, what we learn about ourselves, where our lives take us, and so on. And so we arrive here, where we understand that a lot of witches incorporate bits of different pathways to make their unique niche witchcraft, their personal brand, in other words.

This also comes down to personal understanding. For instance, let's revisit cottage witchery, a part of nature magic. What cottage witchery means to one person may be different to another. Many people associate cottage witchery with the home and everyday magic. But some cottage witches feel the garden plays an integral role in this type of witchery, based on the traditional definition of the cottage—a small living space with a garden that sustains the family. To this person, the cottage witch is defined as having a green thumb.

It's no secret that witchcraft is an inherently subjective practice. It relies on your interpretation of spiritual signs and energy, your understanding of self and your goals, highly personal words written as spells for your situations, and more. This subjectivity means the lines between each type of witchcraft are blurred, and there's no way to prevent that. Even the witch who wants to practice only Scottish witchcraft from the 1800s will find that type of magic, in itself, to be a culmination of change and transformation brought on by humans, who are subjective beings.

We didn't set up this book only to break down its goal of helping you find a path that works. But we did structure it to help you arrive at the core of what makes intermediate witchcraft truly "intermediate": cultivating your path, your niche, based on your knowledge, sense of self, and spiritual journey. Yes, intermediate witchcraft may include more intricate spells, honed skills, and more difficult work, but it's not that clear-cut. Intermediate witchcraft requires us to move beyond definitions and attempting to find ourselves in one of them. It asks us to accept the ambiguity of the spiritual journey and to forge our individual pathway to enlightenment and enchantment.

NICHE WITCHCRAFT

Niche witchcraft, then, is your personal kind of magic, a meld of what you want your spiritual journey and your spell craft to look like. What would niche witchcraft look like? Well, maybe a combination of a good deal of traditional cottage witchery from a certain region, with shadow work and elemental work for healing of the spiritual and physical self. Or perhaps with crystals, textiles, planetary symbols, and more added to develop a protection bottle that sits on your kitchen windowsill, a combination of different types of witchcraft. A lot of witches arrive at this kind of craft, this personalized "niche" practice by way of trying different types of witchery and finding themselves interested in several parts of many, lending to a bit of paralysis in moving forward, halting their witchy journey. That was me.

When I was fourteen, I got my first Book of Shadows and a set of faerie tarot cards. That Book of Shadows would become the bane of my witchy existence, and I would find myself continually going back to it, but out of frustration. I would log information, such as color correspondences and moon phases, as told, but I found that, as I moved along my path, those parts were pointless, because I knew them by heart. This Book of Shadows then, didn't feel like "me" anymore. It felt like an earlier version of me as a witch. Side note: This is the inevitability of a Book of Shadows, because we write information but, inevitably, remember it, rendering the book obsolete. I would rip out pages and start anew. My design choices would change, and so I hated pages I needed because of their look. I would take out parts that didn't interest me much, like having a chart of planetary correspondences to times of day. It just wasn't me. And this led to a pause in my journey. What did I actually practice? Do witches not incorporate planets? What if I don't want to work with deities or spirits? What defines a witch anyway?

Finding these answers requires the witch to understand the subjectivity of witchcraft—in its definition, in its practice and practitioners, in its history and types. And we arrive at the old trusty answer: It depends. It depends on what you want. It depends on what you think witchcraft means. It depends on what you want your path to include. That's vague, but it's in that ambiguity that we understand what intermediate witchcraft is, and can then move into that phase.

I never finished that book. I still have it, but it sits empty, a reminder to me that attempting to define myself and documenting ever-evolving growth was a failure in the making. I was never going to be happy because I was always going to be growing. For you, a Book of Shadows may offer an easy resource and stand as a symbol of your witchy identity. It's a record of your niche path to pass down.

Niche witches are likely to move into writing their own magic rather than relying on books and traditional spells from yesteryear. They want to craft words to match the imagery, aesthetic, feel, and goal of their magic. Cottage witches may reference cobblestones, hedgerows, thickets, and more, whereas the cosmic witch may describe the dance between planets in a bit of waxy poetry used in spell. They may also want to incorporate tools that "feel" like their niche; the crystal witch may have a plethora of crystal jewelry used as protective talismans, whereas the green witch may have a jar of thistles and thorns for that. Tools will vary; the shadow witch may use bones and bog water for healing spells, whereas the home witch may use blankets and dollies. What connects all these witches is their focus on their unique paths.

This focus on the self, this honoring of the self as the guide of their paths, leads the eclectic or niche witch to work with the ideas of overall health and wellness. They understand they are just as much a part of the magic as the world around them, and so they take great care of the self. This likely extends to kin and community, and so the niche or eclectic witch offers wellness and healing to others . . . if they have the energy to share. Remember, this magic, and intermediate magic, in general, is knowing the self and your power, but also knowing when you need to rest and recharge. Because of its specific blend of pathways, eclectic and niche witchcraft is always going to be unique: unique in its inclusions, in its spells, in its spiritual connections, its community support, and more.

A Brief History of Eclectic AND Niche Witchcraft

Although witchcraft is always evolving and changing, and as we discussed in chapter 6, we have the New Age movement to pave the way for eclectic and niche witchcraft, with its broad sense of spirituality as it relates to humanity, and that could be tapped for its spirituality, that interconnectedness, for transformation and healing as part of the wellness journey. Now, practitioners can find their personal path to enlightenment and include whatever they want— astrology, pendulums, spirit boards, tarot, and more—to heighten their spirituality. This à la carte spirituality has, perhaps, grown in the age of hatred of labels and acceptance of self-expression for the sake of personal happiness and well-being. And so it's no surprise that many seeking to express themselves and grow spiritually pick and choose what speaks to them, crafting their pathway to enlightenment and optimum well-being.

Focused Pathway 11
Crystal Witch

Crystals are a common inclusion in spells and rituals for witches of all paths, likely because they are so versatile. Crystals are from earth, speaking to the green witch. They can affect the spiritual self and tether us to divine beings, humanity as a whole, and more, lending to shadow, or psychic, witchery. We use them to charge waters, a go-to practice for water witches. And nearly every occult shop includes gemstones of some sort, so they're easily obtainable.

GETTING STARTED (BEGINNER)

Crystal witches are naturally going to start by developing an arsenal of crystals or stones for a variety of intentions, as each stone has its correspondences, just as plants do. The stone realm is complex, with some "different" stones actually sharing the same materials, such as quartz. As with any interest, the information gets more complex the deeper you delve. If you don't have any stones, clear quartz is the go-to stone for any spell.

Sometimes the witch does nothing more than keep the stone of a certain intention on an altar, in a bag, or as jewelry. Other times, they bury crystals to bury habits, or offer them to the elements as a gift of thanks for support in magic. The use of stones is very versatile, which appeals to the beginner witch testing out different bits of witchcraft that may be ideal for their lifestyle and interests.

We can keep a permanent grid on the altar that acts as a beacon for power and spiritual heightening. Every so often, we can place an item (think: tarot card decks or matchbooks) in the middle of the grid, in place of the anchor stone, to charge it. We can then place the anchor stone on top of the item we put there to further add to its power.

There are many candleholders made of different stones, like amethyst, selenite, and quartz. We can use these with a little tea light to toggle the correspondences to life when we light it. In this way, the elements can work together. The fire kick-starts the intentions of the stone, and the smoke sends it to the universe.

Crystal Energy

Crystals work via their energy. Crystals are considered sources of vibrational energy, but they're also considered conduits for energy, allowing our energy or the energy of the stone's surroundings to infuse the stone and combine with its correspondences. For instance, holding a stone can allow us to remove negativity from ourselves by infusing our negative energy into the stone. Or, we can work with this method backward, for example, holding a stone such as an Amazon River stone or rose quartz to infuse ourselves with the stone's intention, like self-love, confidence, and healing. In these ways, we've transferred energies between ourselves and the stone.

We can also infuse a stone with our messages to a deity or elemental, like gratitude, and bury it in the dirt, toss it in the water, or place it in the space held sacred by that deity to transfer that message. Or, we can have the stone's surroundings infuse the stone. Placing a crystal in water will infuse the water with the stone's power, but also infuse the crystal with the water's power. This is why we set our stones in the moonlight to charge or cleanse them; it's that transference and infusion of energy at work. Many even use stones as the tip of their magical knives, wands, and more to better transfer this energy and infuse their magic with the stone's qualities at the same time.

☘ Crystal Spell for Letting Go

Use this spell when you want to let go of negative thinking, ruminations, or thoughts that keep running through the mind unintentionally.

When to perform this spell:
Saturday, preferably at night when the moon is waning

Ingredients/tools:
Black salt
Black pillar candle
Pin or needle (optional)
Matches or a lighter
Stones: 1 black tourmaline, 1 smoky quartz, 1 amethyst,
  1 jasper of your choosing (there are many kinds)
Muslin bag
Black string or thread

1. Cast a salt circle around the pillar candle. If you'd like, inscribe with the pin a planetary symbol that corresponds to your needs (see pages 142–145), such as the symbol for Uranus (undergoing difficult transitions) or Pluto (banishing or removing), into the candle.

2. Light the candle. Place the tourmaline near the flame. You want the smoke to coat the stone. As you turn the stone in the smoke, state, "To remove the pain that comes with change."

3. Repeat this process with the smoky quartz, but state, "To take the pain with open arms, as it served me well but its role is done."

4. Again, repeat the process with the amethyst, but state, "To remove the stress from a void left open."

5. Last, do this with the jasper, stating, "To fill the void with peace and love."

6. Place the stones in the bag and tie it with black string, ensuring you knot the bag 3 times. (Bonus enchantment: Stitch a cleansing symbol, like a waning moon, on the bag.)

7. Along the southern part of your property, dig a hole in the ground, place the bag in it, and cover it with dirt, carefully patting the ground as you bury it. Use a container pot, if you prefer.

Crystal Charging

Crystals need to be charged and cleansed, especially when using the same stone for different spells. You don't want the residue from old spells to infuse your new work. This requires both cleansing and charging. We want to remove that old energy, but may also want to charge the stone with additional new energy. For instance, if we're trying to encourage business pursuits, but we used our tiger's eye stone in a previous spell for motivation to quit a job, we'll want to cleanse that old energy so the magic doesn't intertwine. We may also want to charge it in the sun to add prosperous energy.

The amount of time it takes to charge a stone depends on who you ask and what you want to use the stone for. For banishing or removing spells, we charge it during the full waning moon period. For additive spells, we charge it in the waxing moon's light. For optimum power to perform any spell, we charge it in the full moon's light, and for newness and change, or dark magic work, we charge it during the new moon. The sun can also charge our stones for prosperity, growth, courage, motivation, and inspiration.

☙ Spell for Charging Stones

This spell is ideally used before any spellwork when you want to use the stone, as stones need time to sit and charge.

When to perform this spell:
Any day, preferably in the morning

Ingredients/tools:
Clear jar, with a lid, full of cleansing brook, stream, or river water

Stone of choice (because not all stones are water safe, do not use calcite, hematite, malachite, pyrite, selenite, or turquoise)

White salt

Matches or a lighter

White chime candle

1. On a Saturday, collect enough water so the stone will be submerged in the same jar you plan to use for this spell.

2. Place the stone into the jar and add a pinch of salt, rotating deosil (clockwise).

3. Seal the lid and give the jar a few easy shakes.

4. Light the candle and pass the smoke around the jar, then "seal" the jar with 9 drops of wax.

5. Place the jar in the moonlight or sunlight for your preferred amount of time, using the information just discussed as a guide.

INTERMEDIATE CRYSTAL WITCHCRAFT

Intermediate witches may want to move beyond simply holding or carrying stones and may prefer to work with the energies of multiple stones to combine intentions for a specific purpose, or use multiple stones to build and direct power. There are several ways to do this, through grids and pyramids.

Crystal Grids

Crystal grids offer a way to centralize and amplify energy while also making our intentions a bit more specific. They rely on geometry to harness and move this energy to the ether, as well as the stones' proximity to each other. Crystal grids, then, are combinations of repetitive, symmetrical patterns of shapes, often circles. These grids look different depending on their intentions. Below is the Flower of Life sacred geometric symbol, and it is one of the most common crystal grid patterns used. However, there many different types of crystal grids that each have unique characteristics.

The stones of the grid depend on your intention, but there is a structure to them. In the center of the grid is an anchor stone. Beyond that are other stones, often placed in concentric circles, that add or modify the intention. Each circle adds a "layer" of intention and the result is a specific goal for the spellwork, radiating outward from the central stone. All stones are placed equidistant from one another so they form a complete circle. You can use color correspondence and stone correspondence to achieve these "layers," or both. Crystal grids can sit anywhere, but it's likely they will sit on an altar or designated space undisturbed for at least a full moon's cycle.

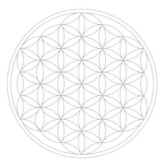

Flower of Life Crystal Grid Pattern

Stones and Their Meanings

STONE	PROPERTIES
Aquamarine, clear quartz, fluorite	Cleansing
Aventurine, calcite, jasper	Healing and grounding
Amazonite, amber, rose quartz	Love
Amethyst, hematite, tourmaline	Negativity removal, banishing
Agate, selenite, turquoise	Peace
Citrine, jade, pyrite	Prosperity
Lapis lazuli, obsidian, tiger's eye	Protection
Abalone shells, emerald, sodalite	Psychic abilities
Celestite, moonstone, sodalite	Spiritual heightening
Carnelian, garnet, onyx	Strength and mental fortitude
Transformation	Labradorite, malachite, obsidian

❧ Crystal Grid Spell for Healing

We can use crystal grids to help our healing. Because healing is a multifaceted concept, healing spellwork is nuanced. Crystal grids provide the ability to "layer" different aspects of healing needed for overall well-being, like self-love, patience, and calm. This spell uses a power stone, love stones, strength stones, and peace stones to encourage those intentions.

When to perform this spell:
Sunday 1 p.m. or 8 p.m.

Ingredients/tools:
Crystal grid of choice
Matches or a lighter
Cleansing herb bundles, such as mint or thyme
1 large quartz stone
6 rose quartz stones
6 carnelian stones
6 selenite stones (optional)

1. Place a crystal grid on your altar or other spiritual space.
2. Light your cleansing herb bundle to purify the space.
3. Place your large quartz stone in the center of the grid as the anchor.
4. Place each rose quartz stone around the anchor, forming a circle.
5. Place the carnelian stones around the rose quartz stones, in the outermost tertiary circumference of the grid, forming a circle.
6. Place the selenite stones (if using) between the carnelian stones. You can either let the grid sit until the spell manifests, within a full moon's cycle, or when you want to do another spell, or when your intuition tells you that it's time to take the grid down.

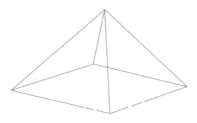

Witches' Pyramid

Using the Witches' Pyramid

A witches' pyramid is a pyramid made of metal rods like the one above, or it can also be fully enclosed. You can place stones, or other items, inside the pyramid or at each corner (inside or outside the pyramid) to centralize the energies of those items so they flow upward and outward. This also helps build power within the pyramid, and much like a circle, the witch can do her spells within the borders of that pyramid for optimum power and protection. Witches' pyramids are usually made of metal, and that metal has a correspondence. Iron is protective, whereas copper is healing. Gold holds a sacred quality that corresponds to spiritual connection and divinity.

⚘ Witches' Pyramid Spell to Build Power

Use this spell when you want to charge an item with the powers of stones, or when you want to build power for a spell.

When to perform this spell:
Sunday or Monday, when the moon is full

Ingredients/tools:
Stones of choice (depending on the kind of power you'd like to build)
Witches' pyramid, in iron or gold
Matches or a lighter
Dried thyme or mint cleansing bundle
Full moon water
Item to charge, such as a book, piece of jewelry, or candle

1. Place your stones within the pyramid so they're touching.

2. Light the bundle and move it around the perimeter of the pyramid along the bottom. Then, at each corner, move the bundle from the corner to the apex of the pyramid. You have now cleansed the pyramid as well as enhanced the space with power.

3. Repeat the same order of movement but now with the moon water. Dip a finger in the moon water and go around the perimeter of the pyramid with it, and then touch each corner, venturing up to the apex each time.

4. Take both hands and place them along the left and right sides of the pyramid, and then move them upward to move the power.

5. Now, you can hold an item, like a piece of jewelry or a Book of Shadows, above the pyramid to absorb the power; you could hold a picture of the self there; or you could charge candles by holding them at the apex, too. You could even perform a spell using the sacred space within the four corners of the base of the pyramid. It is up to you. The prism of power is built in this space and above it.

Focused Pathway 12
Wellness Witch

One could argue that all witchcraft is meant to bring about some sort of wellness, be it spiritual, physical, or emotional. But the wellness witch puts their well-being at the forefront of their practice. This means that healing, confidence, self-love, and comfort are of particular focus. The wellness witch may also bring other types of witchery into their practice. As we've learned by our journey through this book, the beauty of witchcraft and its different paths is that they connect and collide with one another. The wellness witch likely dabbles in kitchen witchery when working with comforting teas to bring rest and relaxation, or may incorporate restorative tonics in those teas or place them under the tongue for added herbal support. The wellness witch may incorporate yoga or meditation into their practice to add to their spiritual well-being, or they may even teach it to provide wellness to others. We may find that poetry guides a lot of the spellwork, or that other expressions of self permeate this pathway. The wellness witch may craft paintings or pottery, perform interpretive dances or make music as a means to express emotion and manifest intention. After all, the conscious swiping of brush to canvas builds just as much power as inscribing symbols in wax or braiding textiles.

Gray candles represent the shadow, but they also represent the true nature of any being. Good and bad, dark and light. Both aspects come together to make us who we are. Gray candles embody that idea and breathe life into both parts. If you don't have gray candles, black and white ones work, as well as any healing or stabilizing colors, such as brown, dark green, and lavender. You might burn the candle before any meditation to meet the self, to symbolize "lighting the pathway" to the shadow.

Protective sigils or healing sigils can be personal to you and made by combining the letters of healing words (or your name) into a symbol. Follow your intuition in crafting them. Inscribe these into symbols in your candle.

A mix of dried marigold or calendula petals and thyme offer prophetic yet restful dreams and help build psychic abilities. Craft an anointing oil mixture out of them with evening primrose carrier oil and apply it to a candle.

The moon represents the subconscious, and it's the entity or celestial body we invoke for work related to emotions, dreams, intuition, and hidden shadows

that influence us. The moon might also represent the goddess(es) or entities we want to invoke, like maiden, mother, or crone, for their spiritual wisdom and support in our shadow journeys. To create moon water, collect spring water (or clean snow) during the waxing crescent moon to harness the elements of the maiden (bravery, courage, vitality). Collect water in the full moon for optimum power and to connect to the goddess in her mother state—comforting, all-powerful, in control, strong, guiding. Collect water during a waning moon to harness the qualities of the crone—wisdom, guidance, comfort, and calm strength. Dab this water on your temples, third eye, and the base of your neck (front and back) before any meditation.

For the wellness witch, the self is also an altar, a sacred space that honors the spiritual self and houses magic. Amulets with animals or stones that have strength and courage as their main intention are helpful to wear. Bears, buffalo, deer or elk, roosters, wolves, and wrens are ideal animals for this purpose. For healing and transformation, select snakes. You can also choose more docile animals, such as the hare, mice, or swallow, who have a cunning and sly, yet tiny, nature about them. These spiritual beings represent healing, cleverness, softness, and the ability to survive adversity.

GETTING STARTED: HEALING AND EMPOWERING (BEGINNER)

The wellness witch may find this particular path due to a need for healing, be it emotional, spiritual, or physical. And so we begin there. Healing is such an umbrella term, but we can think of it as being mindful of what the self needs, and holding those needs important every day. This often includes checking in with the self at various times of day to ensure needs are being met, to sit with the self when emotions arise to regulate them via internal (or external) dialogue, placing boundaries on work and others to ensure we get what we need, such as rest. The list is endless and, often times, is not "magical" in any way. These are everyday things we can do to support our general well-being.

What makes these magical, then, is bringing in what we've learned in this book to identify magical correspondences, speak to the elements, converse with spirits and with our intuition, acknowledge the shadows and our place among the cosmos, and take care of our sacred spaces for optimum wellness. Although you don't have to incorporate all these ideas, you may be inclined to incorporate some of them.

Healing Intentions

Healing is an intention all by itself, but when we talk about performing "healing magic," we could be talking about a variety of things: physical ailments or emotional upheavals. But even within that context, there are nuances. Are you trying to heal deep anxieties? Issues of self-worth? Negative self-talk? Breakup blues? Familial issues? Past traumas? There are so many facets of healing, and each deserves a focus. The following are some spells to support some specific intentions, but when you move into crafting your own, break down what it is you mean by "healing."

❦ "Blanket Chest" Tea for Healing and Comfort

The perfect place to begin with healing magic is with comforting teas. Whether it's the warmth of the liquid or the melding of herbs with healing intention, teas never fail to offer a bit of comfort in hard times.

When to perform this spell:
Any day at any time

Ingredients/tools:
One 16-ounce (475 ml) Mason jar
3 tablespoons (6 g) loose Ceylon tea
1 tablespoon whole coriander seeds
1 teaspoon aniseed
2 fresh rosemary leaves
½ teaspoon ground coriander
2 cups (475 ml) hot water
Sweetener of choice (optional)

1. In the Mason jar, combine the tea, coriander seeds, aniseed, rosemary, coriander, and hot water. Let steep for 5 minutes. Add sweetener to taste (if using).

2. As you stir widdershins (counterclockwise) the tea, breathe into the cup and meld your breath with the steam of the tea. These collide as they rise into the air, connecting you to the healing and protective properties of the tea. Whisper, "Relief begins as I hush the tongue. I take in the healing, let go of what is done."

❧ Resilience Spell for Hardships

Perform this spell when you need to overcome adversity or face obstacles, internal or external, that you don't necessarily want to face.

When to perform this spell:
Thursday or Sunday, at noon when the moon is waxing

Ingredients/tools:
White salt or sand
Earthenware dish
Gold pillar candle
Dried tea leaves of choice and borage*
Pine essential oil, or an essential oil of one of the "clarity" herbs: mint,
    summer savory, lemon leaf or peel, or lavender (see page 64)
Carrier oil of choice (see page 64)
Matches or a lighter
Obsidian stone
Small muslin or leather sachet

1. Place the salt in the earthenware dish and nestle the candle in the salt, making sure it is stable.

2. Sprinkle some of the tea leaves and borage into the dish, working deosil (clockwise).

3. Anoint the candle with the oil mixture and light it.

4. Hold the obsidian in your dominant hand. Close your eyes and focus on the breath. Envision hedge thorns emerging from your skin, slowly yet deliberately. In some parts of the skin grow thick brambles and leggy hedges, or bushes with flowers of your choice. Envision beautiful bits of bark shielding the skin, drifting over the arms and legs protectively. As you inhale, take in the heat and dry air from the sun; as you exhale, envision yourself pushing out the obstacle into the air, and watch it float into the sun.

*Safety Note: *The leaves of borage can be mildly toxic to people and pets.*

Now state:

> "As Daedalus's son, I venture close but the wings cast shields and spires.
> As Icarus's father, I watch and wait; the sun, my son, goes higher.
> He catches the rays and within him stays a humble warrior kneeling.
> I conjure the strength to face the day, and challenge the woes I'm feeling.
> I pull from the pain; I find skill in the strain.
> I conquer the shadows of healing.
> I rewrite my son's fate, I conjure the sun's rays,
> yet bow to the beams that I'm shielding."

5. When ready, place the remainder of the tea leaves and borage into the sachet, along with the stone, and carry this with you.

Self Magic

The wellness witch focuses on the self in order to fill the inner cup with happiness and healthiness. It may sound corny, but this focus on the self makes sure we're okay enough to care for others who need us. But more than that, this self magic makes sure any shadows within, or any self-doubts, are approached with kindness and compassion so the self, as a whole, feels at peace. Self magic varies. It can include the healing magic just discussed, or external wellness of community building or spiritual connections discussed following. It can include a bit of protection for the self so any external issues don't impact our sense of self. But, sometimes, the simplest bits of self magic simply allow the self to "be." To rest. To sit. To be passive. There is magic in all actions we include in spellwork, but there is equal magic in allowing ourselves to simply observe the world. It's a different kind of magic, one that manifests internal care.

⚘ Cord Magic for Negativity Removal

Use this spell to find release from internal energies, be they from a person, a situation, or a spirit. Working with cords allows us to infuse our negative energies into the cord, thereby getting them out of the self.

When to perform this spell:
Saturday or Thursday at 11 p.m.

Ingredients/tools:
Scissors
Fabric bits that speak to the happy, lighter side of you
   (favorite colors or patterns)
Fabric bits that are darker and more earthy
White cord
Black cord
Gray ribbon (or a softer texture than cord)
Salt (any kind)
8 bells, ideally copper, with loops at the top for hanging

1. Cut the fabric pieces into strips the length you want your resulting cord to be. A good measure is about 12 inches (30 cm).

2. Cut your white and black cords the same length as the fabric strips.

3. Cut the gray ribbon at 9½ inches (24 cm).

4. Bundle the strips together and tie a knot at the top, so the bits of fabric, cords, and ribbon hang loosely.

5. Sprinkle salt around your work area.

6. Begin braiding the cord. Place the white cord and "positive" bits of fabric on the left side. Position the gray ribbon in the middle. Place the black cord and darker bits of fabric on the right side. Braid down about 1 inch (2.5 cm). Once there, tie a bell with the gray fabric. State, "Bell of one: I weave the cord and start the spell."

7. Repeat this pattern 7 more times (8 times total), stating the corresponding line of the following incantation when tying each remaining bell:

   "Bell of two: The darkness swells to rise up the well."
   "Bell of three: It glides over the cobbles and meets the earth."
   "Bell of four: She drinks the elixir with humbled mirth."
   "Bell of five: She absorbs the darkness that dims the path."
   "Bell of six: And eases the pains that ache to last."
   "Bell of seven: A swift, gentle breeze as she eases within."
   "Bell of eight: Acknowledges what a godsend my darkness has been."

8. Tie a final knot and state:

   "A moon takes both light and dark to evolve.
   The earth knows in balance is where hardships dissolve.
   I weave these traits and in my bones, they dance about in tandem.
   I let the dark flow with the light, with the grace and love gray hands them."

9. Hang this cord outside your home, or in a personal space where you experience negativity.

Rest Magic

Rest magic encourages the mind to steady itself and become a bit passive rather than feeling as though it always has to take part and make decisions. This is less "sleep" rest and more the kind of rest we need to recharge and reset ourselves on stressful days.

☘ Meditation for Healing and Rest

Meditations are great for healing in that they ask you to go inward and be with yourself. They ask you to use your skills of self-soothing and comforting, and even if you're not expert at that, you're trying. A good meditation for healing begins with identifying a healing energy and coating yourself in it. We will elaborate more on this when we discuss the idea of our inner, younger selves (see page 198). Perform this meditation when the mind needs a bit of a break, and the heart needs a bit of tranquility.

When to perform this spell:
Sunday, any time (8 p.m. or 11 p.m. are ideal)

Ingredients/tools:
None

1. Steady your mind with a good 4-4-4 breath: Inhale for 4 seconds, hold for 4 seconds, and exhale for 4 seconds.

2. Next, hum to yourself, any notes you like, but use a comforting, soft hum.

3. Envision yourself surrounded by and sitting in snow, yet you're shielded from its cold. Around you, snow is falling, but it's frozen in place. Nothing is moving. Find comfort in this frozen time; you've carved out this time as healing time for yourself. Take in what you've imagined to be your environment, with the soft hum in the background. As you continue, let time speed up a little, as the snow begins to fall ever so slightly. The trees move gently in the wind. That's your power doing that.

4. This gentle breeze stirs the snowfall, and the snow builds on itself until it creates a thick cotton quilt. This quilt falls on your shoulders from above. It wraps around your body as you sit and hum. An animal stirs in the tree line, and you spot it. What animal is it? Note this symbolism later.

5. Feel the warmth of this blanket coat your skin. Your hum enchants the snow and it begins falling at normal speed. The trees move naturally as well. All is soft, silent. There's a fire in the distance, and its smoke billows upward. You smell the ancestral smoke and sense the warmth of the flame. That smoke drifts over you and falls downward. Let it comfort you, too. That's the presence of your spiritual lineage. This smoke dances and moves like our ancestors would if they were still among us—living, warm, human. But they are alive and free in the otherworld, and they've drifted over to coddle you.

6. Find peace here with them. Find warmth and comfort from the smells and the spiritual weight of the blanket. Speak to the ancestors, if you feel called to. If you've stopped humming, start again.

7. Once you feel a sense of internal calm, it's time to come back to the present. Hyperfocus on your humming and the vibrations in your throat. Make your humming louder to wake up the physical body. If you ventured mentally into this snow-laden space a certain way, by a pathway or following an animal, follow the path or animal out exactly as you came in. If you didn't, begin wiggling your toes and fingers.

8. Lastly, open your eyes and take in your surroundings.

9. Consider noting the following. All these are symbols for you to interpret.

    ◆ What kinds of trees were around you?

    ◆ What time of day was it?

    ◆ Were you some place you recognized, like a grandparent's yard?

    ◆ What was the animal you spied at the tree line?

    ◆ Were there birds or other animals?

    ◆ What color clothes were you wearing?

    ◆ Did your blanket manifest in a color other than white

INTERMEDIATE WELLNESS WITCHCRAFT

The intermediate wellness witch is going to step a bit beyond the safety and comfort of the conscious self and is likely to venture into "What's next? What's beyond this?" This goes two ways. One way delves even deeper into the self for deep healing and complete well-being, not just at the conscious level. The other way looks outward, beyond the self, to see how the self connects and relates to something larger than itself. And so, intermediate wellness magic is for the well-versed witch.

Internal Wellness

Like any eclectic path, a multitude of practices populates each pathway, and the wellness witch understands that internal wellness moves beyond emotions in the present. Because of that understanding, this witchery is likely to include intermediate shadow work, such as focusing on the different parts of the self with a conscious effort to integrate those selves into a happy being. Often times, shadow work becomes imperative, almost a necessity, because we feel fragmented; we have different parts of ourselves that feel separate from each other, be it in personality or wants and needs. How can we feel whole rather than just simply the sum of our memories?

☫ Shadow Work Spell to Combine the Self

Combining the fragmented parts of self is often a job left to professionals, and rightfully so. It's dangerous work since we're dealing with inner identities that feel disconnected from one another. Or we may simply want the inner child or angsty teenager in us to feel soothed by who we are now. No matter our goal, we can support our journey to find interconnectedness with a bit of magic. Remember, shadow work (see pages 156–169) is dangerous, since it asks us to be in the right state of mind and grounded in reality so that we don't think of ourselves as separate people in one body. Mentioning professional support is a must.

When to perform this spell:
Any day, preferably around dinnertime

Ingredients/tools:

Bowl of salt

Plate or shallow dish

Varied herbs (see descriptions in step 2)

Various biodegradable items, such as threads or pictures,
   which represent parts of the self (see descriptions in step 2)

Water (tumbled water is ideal)

1. Separate the salt into individual piles on a plate or a dish. The number of piles should represent the fragments of self, so your amount may vary from someone else's.

2. Add some herbs to each pile. Your choices may correspond to that fragment of self's personality, interests, or age. Choose thyme, mint, or lavender for a child; elderflower for old age; willow, pansy, or loosestrife for the self who is grieving; willow catkins for our time as a mother; and so on. Color magic may also come into play: Threads with a color significance can be added to the pile. We may choose red or orange for the businessperson inside, or purple and blue may represent our spiritual self or higher self. Whatever goes into these salt piles needs to be biodegradable.

3. As you craft each salt pile, envision yourself as that fragment—a lost child, alone in the room, for instance, or a mother who is running ragged and stressed. Whatever those iterations are for you, envision each and give each the time, respect, and honor it deserves. They were you when you were doing the best you could. After you envision this person, touch the corresponding pile and state, "I see you."

4. After all piles have been honored, go around the circle again, transferring each pile into the main bowl of salt. As you do this for each pile, state, "I know you."

5. After all piles are transferred, add enough water to the bowl to cover the salt, and stir deosil (clockwise) with your finger (use a glove if needed). Let the salt intermingle and dissolve. It is best if this water is slow, tumbled brook or creek water, but any water will do. Once the salt and water begin to combine, state, "I feel you within the whole of self." Envision the parts coming together and integrating; the colors combining to make beautiful new colors. The salts meld with each other. And as they stir in the mind's eye, they take shape, slowly creating you as you are. Look at yourself once you're created. See yourself. State, "As above, so below. As the one I've come to know."

6. See yourself encapsulated in a white aura. The self is swirling and moving with colors and textures and bits of memory. Nod to this person and open your eyes. Pour this water along the northern side of the home, grounding it in the foundation where it needs to grow.

External Wellness

External wellness can come in a variety of ways. Like most intermediate subjects, things get a bit more abstract and ambiguous the deeper we delve into them. What does external wellness mean? It could refer to external wellness as the well-being of the physical self, and this may include practicing exercises or physical movements that hold a spiritual undertone, like yoga or tai chi. These exercises help us connect the mind, body, and spirit, offering an alignment that may encourage overall spiritual wellness.

External wellness can also refer to a feeling of duty to community. An intermediate wellness witch may feel inclined to support the well-being of others just as they support theirs. They understand that their knowledge can be used to help others in their journeys, and so they may offer the community wellness items like healing salves, charms for strength and hope, and so on. The kind of offerings aren't the focus; rather, it's the movement from working on the self to extending those thoughts outward to others.

External wellness can also be interpreted as seeing ourselves as part of an external whole. This might be the small tethers to a larger community, or it could refer to our place as one spiritual being amid all the cosmos. This may include spells and rituals that strengthen those connections and honor them, which help us see ourselves as part of something bigger, as something integral to the universe.

✤ Wholeness Spell

Sometimes, to feel better, we simply need to be reminded that we are part of a collective conscious, something bigger than ourselves that we contribute to in a meaningful way. In this interconnectedness, we see additional purpose for ourselves, and find peace knowing others carry the same personal shadows; they just look, sound, and feel different.

When to perform this spell:
Friday, when the moon is full or nearing full

Ingredients/tools:

Inscription tool

Large white pillar candle

Grapeseed carrier oil mixed with an essential oil of the one of the "clarity"
  herbs: mint, summer savory, lemon leaf or peel, or lavender (and sweetgrass, optional); see page 64

Matches or a lighter

Cradle of humankind stone (optional)

1. Inscribe a deep circle into the candle, and then anoint that circle with the oil
    mixture. Rub the oil mixture, deosil (clockwise), around the perimeter of the circle,
    and then light the candle. Place a drip of the oil into the wax pool of the candle's
    flame. As you do, say:

    > "As above, so below.
    > Wholeness seeks to drink the woe.
    > I hold the hands of heathen strength,
    > find the words to conjure faith,
    > speak to those who've endured the same,
    > connect to bones of Mother's name.
    > But mothers cannot bear relentless pain,
    > so wholeness soaks what mother can't.
    > I connect to the ether, the ancestor, the mother, the whole
    > the spirit in otherworlds above and below.
    > They guide me and find me, the shadows in the sun.
    > And in connecting to each, we are but just one."

2. Let the candle burn and envision roots shooting out from your body in all direc-
    tions, latching on like tethers to the world around you, be it the trees outside or the
    carpet inside.

3. If you like, for added support, soak a cradle of humankind stone in tumbled water
    and leave in the full moon's cycle. Strain or take the stone out of the water. The
    water can be tossed into a container pot or garden. Extinguish the candle. Then,
    carry the stone with you to feel connected to the collective whenever you begin
    to feel isolated.

CONCLUSION

In this book, each chapter highlights the various kinds of witchery you may encounter, and each topic has been explored by scholars and practitioners. There is no shortage of this information available. What we hope is apparent here is that there is overlap and nuance to the concept of identity and who we are as people, not just as witches. We may seek out labels and categories to find ourselves, but when we delve deeper, we learn those labels and categories don't mean anything; they overlap and dance together. They collide and beg for attention. Some slip away quietly while others take a foothold in our practice. And, as we age, this all shifts based on our interests, our environment, and who we are as people.

Just like identity in general, we're always shifting our witchy identity, and so the question is: Does it matter what you call yourself? Does any term you choose change the definition of who you are just because you worded your title a certain way? The beginner witch may find comfort in finding themselves among the categories, but intermediate witches know that those categories, ultimately, don't matter, because who you are as a witch doesn't need a definition or a title to exist. Call yourself any title you'd like, as intricate as you like! But understand that the title of "witch" is enough. You're a part of the community regardless, and you're safe here no matter your path.

ACKNOWLEDGMENTS

There are many people who had their hands in the production of this book either directly or indirectly, and their support in making this book come to life is priceless. First, I'd like to thank John Foster, whose guidance and editorial work provided valuable feedback and honed my skills as a writer. That thanks extends to Weldon Owen for the opportunity to craft this book.

I'd also like to thank my colleagues at *Witchology Magazine*, who provided support and camaraderie while writing this book, not to mention the opportunity to snuggle into the world of editing and witchery and perform work that I love. Their continued guidance as we venture through each magazine issue has been a steady source of confidence, and my position has afforded me many awesome opportunities. Thank you.

I truly cannot thank Ambrosia Hawthorn enough for reaching out and asking me to edit *Witchology Magazine* years ago, for asking me to write this book alongside her, and for each awesome idea we developed together and tried to materialize. All of this changed my life and allowed me to learn, grow and explore more of the witchy and publishing communities. I will forever be grateful and indebted. I could not ask for a kinder, more helpful colleague.

Many thanks go to Steve, whose presence and support helped validate my thoughts and see the positive in work and in life when it was hard. Your emotional support pulled me out of many blocks and back into these pages.

I'd like to thank my dad, whose love for writing and crafting creative things mirrors my own. For every piece of my teenage poetry still being found in old dresser drawers, there is a long-lost page of song lyrics scribbled on pieces of paper by a younger man who also found solace in words. Each news article, column article, composition lecture—and now each incantation and book page—could not have been written without the invaluable support and truly unconditional love from the best Poose. I am honored to receive such love.

Last, to my daughter Winnie, who fills my life with hope. You are truly sunshine manifested, and your love and kindness always inspire me in everything I do. This book could not have been written without your encouraging little face and your bright tresses dancing with the wind.

About the Authors

Ambrosia Hawthorn is a tarot reader, astrologer, and traveling eclectic witch with roots in Yup'ik shamanism and Puerto Rican folk magic. She is the owner of Wild Goddess Magick, a witchcraft blog, and the editorial director of *Witchology Magazine*. Ambrosia's goal is to create and share new content about all types of magic with every witch.

Sarah Justice is the managing editor of *Witchology Magazine* and contributing writer for *Lisa Chamberlain's Witches' Planners* for 2021 and 2022. She also owns The Tiny Cauldron (tinycauldron.com), an online witchcraft cottage filled with enchanted ritual items and kits to help witches foster their magic. Sarah's craft expertise focuses on Appalachian folk magick, cottage witchery, and colonial American folk practices.

INDEX

weldon**owen**

an imprint of Insight Editions
P.O. Box 3088
San Rafael, CA 94912
www.weldonowen.com

CEO Raoul Goff
VP Publisher Roger Shaw
Editorial Director Katie Killebrew
Senior Editor John Foster
Editor Claire Yee
Editorial Assistant Kayla Belser
VP Creative Chrissy Kwasnik
Art Director Ashley Quackenbush
Senior Designer Stephanie Odeh
VP Manufacturing Alix Nicholaeff
Sr Production Manager Joshua Smith
Sr Production Manager, Subsidiary Rights Lina s Palma-Temena

Chapters 1 to 3 © 2023 Ambrosia Hawthorn
Chapter 3 to 7 by 2023 Sarah Justice
Illustrations © 2023 Travis Stewart

Weldon Owen would also like to thank Mary Cassells for copyediting,
Leslie S. Jacoby for proofreading, and Timothy Griffin for indexing.

ISBN: 978-1-68188-890-3

Manufactured in China by Insight Editions

10 9 8 7 6 5 4 3 2

ROOTS of PEACE
REPLANTED PAPER

Insight Editions, in association with Roots of Peace, will plant two trees for each tree used in the manufacturing of
this book. Roots of Peace is an internationally renowned humanitarian organization dedicated to eradicating land
mines worldwide and converting war-torn lands into productive farms and wildlife habitats. Roots of Peace will plant
two million fruit and nut trees in Afghanistan and provide farmers there with the skills and support necessary for
sustainable land use.